Introduction to Healthcare Information
Enabling Technologies

Edited by

Raymond A. Gensinger, Jr., MD, CPHIMS, FHIMSS

D1517142

HIMSS Mission

To lead healthcare transformation through effective use of health information technology.

Printed in the U.S.A. 5 4 3 2 1

Requests for permission to make copies of any part of this work should be sent to:
Permissions Editor
HIMSS
230 E. Ohio, Suite 500
Chicago, IL 60611-3269
nvitucci@himss.org

ISBN 978-0-9821070-5-8

For more information about HIMSS, please visit www.himss.org.

About the Editor

Raymond A. Gensinger, Jr., MD, CPHIMS, FHIMSS, is the Chief Medical Information Officer (CMIO) for Fairview Health Services, an integrated delivery network, in Minnesota. Dr. Gensinger is also a general internist and holds appointments as an Assistant Professor of Internal Medicine, as Affiliate Faculty of the School of Nursing, and as Faculty of the Institute for Health Informatics, all at the University of Minnesota. Dr. Gensinger is an associate of the American College of Physicians, a Fellow of the Healthcare Information and Management Systems Society (HIMSS), and a Certified Professional in Healthcare Information and Management Systems (CPHIMS).

As CMIO for Fairview, Dr. Gensinger is responsible for the clinical information technology transformation strategy for the organization. He has held similar roles at the Hennepin County Medical Center in Minneapolis. At Fairview, Dr. Gensinger chairs the Clinical Governance Steering Committee, as well as provides oversight for all other clinical information acquisitions and decisions made at Fairview.

The Past Chair of the Minnesota Epic Users Group and the Chair Elect for the Minnesota Health Information Exchange, Dr. Gensinger serves on the Minnesota e-Health Initiative Advisory Committee. He is a Past President for the Minnesota Chapter of HIMSS and is a former member of the HIMSS Board of Directors. Dr. Gensinger has authored or presented on over 50 different healthcare information systems related topics and received the Healthcare Informatics Innovator Award in September 2006 from *Healthcare Informatics* magazine.

As an undergraduate at Illinois Wesleyan University, Dr. Gensinger studied biology. He moved to Southern Illinois University (SIU) School of Medicine for his medical school, internship and residency training. During medical school and residency, Dr. Gensinger was involved in medical education and the development of a Problem Based Learning Curriculum. After residency, he served as a Chief of Residents in Internal Medicine, followed by two years of service on the clinical faculty at SIU. In 1994, part of Dr. Gensinger's time was spent at the Baylor College of Medicine, Houston, where he pursued postdoctoral studies in Medical Informatics.

About the Contributors

Marion J. Ball, EdD, FACMI, FCHIME, FHIMSS, FAAN, is the Senior Advisor, Healthcare and Life Sciences Institute for IBM Research. Dr. Ball is Professor Emerita at Johns Hopkins University School of Nursing, and a faculty member in the Division of Health Sciences Informatics at Johns Hopkins School of Medicine. She is a member of the Institute of Medicine and serves on the Board of Regents of the National Library of Medicine. Dr. Ball also serves on a variety of boards in the area of health information technology, including serving as president of the International Medical Informatics Association (IMIA), and as a board member of the American Medical Informatics Association (AMIA) and the American Health Information Management Association Foundation (AHIMA/FORE), and co-chair of the Healthcare Information and Management Systems Society (HIMSS) Board of Directors. She received the Morris F. Collen Lifetime Achievement Award from AMIA, and is an honorary member of Sigma Theta Tau, the Honor Society of Nursing, and the Medical Library Association (MLA). Most recently, Dr. Ball was inducted as an Honorary Fellow of the American Academy of Nursing (AAN). She is the author/editor of more than 20 books and over 260 articles in the field of health informatics. Her book, *Consumer Informatics,* received the HIMSS 2005 Book-of-the-Year Award. Her book *Nursing Informatics: Where Caring and Technology Meet* has most recently been translated into Chinese and Portuguese, joining the family of other translations into Japanese, German, Korean, and Polish. The *4th Edition* of *Nursing Informatics: Where Caring and Technology Meet* will be published in 2010.

Melinda Yates Costin is Vice President of Baylor Health Care System. With over 35 years of healthcare experience, Ms. Costin has spent most of those years developing and implementing products supporting the electronic health record concept. She has served the healthcare industry in the provider, vendor and consulting environments, focusing on process design and change management that enhances care quality. Accomplishments of note over the course of Ms. Costin's career include: the implementation of a full clinical system at a 500-bed hospital in the mid-1970s, one of the first automated patient records and a demonstration site for the efforts of many other organizations; the development and implementation of one of the first electronic medical records for the Department of Defense; and the development and implementations of clinical rules packages, in conjunction with Intermountain Health Care. She has led implementations of both ambulatory and inpatient systems in both the private and government sectors, and mentored many clinicians in using their combined clinical and technical knowledge to improve the environment for healthcare delivery. Ms. Costin has lectured at many well known health IT events including events sponsored by HIMSS, the College of

Healthcare Information Management Executives (CHIME), Towards An Electronic Patient Record (TEPR), and AMIA. In addition, she spoke at the International Congress in Nursing Informatics in Rio de Janeiro, Brazil and the Medical Informatics Europe conference in Geneva, Switzerland.

Donna B. DuLong, BSN, RN, is a health IT consultant. Ms. DuLong has worked in the healthcare IT industry for 20 years, focusing primarily on nursing-based, IT solutions related to patient safety, medication management, and evidence-based knowledge. She led the Technology Informatics Guiding Education Reform (TIGER) Initiative for two years as executive director, coordinating the efforts of the nine collaborative teams and the participating organizations toward achieving the three-year action plan that was defined at the TIGER Summit in 2006. Ms. DuLong has held several executive management positions in the healthcare IT market with responsibilities for business development, product development and management, marketing, compliance, implementation, and customer support.

Kent L. Gale, is the Founder and Chairman of the Board of KLAS Enterprises LLC. Mr. Gale founded KLAS in 1996 when it was obvious that unbiased reporting of client satisfaction was missing from the health IT industry. He has been deeply involved in health IT for 35 years, serving healthcare providers (Intermountain Healthcare), software vendors (Medlab, Sunquest, 3M, GTE, Compucare) and research/consulting organizations both nationally and internationally. Mr. Gale is a graduate of Brigham Young University, and has lived in Brazil, Germany and the Philippines. He has traveled worldwide exploring the use of health IT and is a frequent presenter at national and international conferences. He is a former member of the CHIME Board of Trustees and recipient of CHIME's 2006 Lifetime Achievement Award. Currently a member of CHIME and HIMSS, Mr. Gale has also presented at HIMSS National Meetings and HIMSS Regional Seminars. He was formerly a member of HISSG and SCAMC, and has been affiliated with ECHO, an IBM Health Industry Professional Association. Mr. Gale is currently serving on the CHIME Education Foundation Board.

George T. (Buddy) Hickman, FHIMSS, CPHIMS, is Executive Vice President and Chief Information Officer (CIO) for Albany Medical Center in New York's Capital Region. As a health industry veteran, he has held several senior healthcare industry and academic provider posts, namely as CIO. Prior to joining Albany Med, Mr. Hickman was a partner with Ernst & Young LLP's healthcare consulting practice and worked earlier in his career with Price Waterhouse. He started his work in healthcare as a project engineer for a health provider. Mr. Hickman has performed consulting engagements across the United States as well as for the Ministry of Health in Singapore and the United Kingdom Health Authority. He is a past board chair, nominating committee chair, and a Fellow for HIMSS; a past board member for HIMSS Analytics; a charter member of the College of Healthcare Information Management Executives (CHIME); and the National Liaison for the HIMSS New York State Chapter. Mr. Hickman was honored as the recipient of the 2007 CHIME-HIMSS John E. Gall CIO of the Year Award. He sits on the board of the Health Information Exchange for New York (HIXNY). A frequent speaker and lecturer on a variety of health IT-related topics, Mr. Hickman has published extensively on a variety of health IT-related topics, including co-authoring *The Healthcare Information Technology Planning Fieldbook*, published by HIMSS.

Larry Kryzaniak, FHFMA, joined Hennepin County Medical Center in February of 2004 as its Chief Financial Officer. Prior to HCMC, Mr. Kryzaniak spent 25 years with Allina Health System and its predecessor organizations. While with Allina, he served in nearly every financial position in the organization, finishing up as the interim chief financial officer. In these positions, he was able to experience numerous financial turnaround opportunities, was the lead in approximately $1 billion in financings, numerous financial system changes and negotiated numerous acquisitions and divestitures. Mr. Kryzaniak holds a Masters Degree in Management and is certified as a Fellow in Healthcare Financial Management.

T. Douglas Lawson serves as the President of Baylor Regional Medical Center at Grapevine, a 249-bed acute care facility. This hospital offers advanced medical care for more than 20 cities throughout the Dallas/Fort Worth Metroplex. During Mr. Lawson's tenure at Baylor, the hospital has received numerous state and national awards, including the Baldrige-based Texas Award for Performance Excellence in 2009 and the 2009 Texas Health Care Quality Improvement Award of Excellence. His solid strategic operational management has led to controlled costs, increased operating income in excess of 10% and consistently enhanced results during a period where he orchestrated over $81 million in hospital expansion projects. Named a 2008 Healthcare Hero by the *Dallas Business Journal*, Mr. Lawson is a highly regarded healthcare leader who has consistently driven exemplary results throughout his 17-year healthcare tenure. In addition to Baylor, he has held progressively responsible leadership roles at M.D. Anderson, Saint Luke's Health System and Cabell Huntington Hospital.

Judy Murphy, RN, FACMI, FHIMSS, has held national prominence as a health IT executive, leader in the nursing informatics community, and a much sought after speaker for health informatics conferences for 25 years. She is Vice President, IT Applications, at Aurora Health Care in Wisconsin, an integrated delivery network with 14 hospitals, 120 ambulatory centers, home health agencies, and 28,000 employees. Ms. Murphy oversees all application software supporting clinical and business operations at Aurora's acute care facilities and is project executive for Aurora's electronic health record initiative. She has published and lectured nationally and internationally on system implementation methodologies, automated clinical documentation, and the use of technology to support evidence-based practice. Ms. Murphy served on the AMIA Board of Directors and will begin serving on the HIMSS Board of Directors in July, 2010. She is a Fellow of both the American College of Medical Informatics and HIMSS. She received the 2006 HIMSS Nursing Informatics Leadership Award, and was named one of the "20 People Who Make Healthcare Better" in 2007 by *HealthLeaders* magazine. Ms. Murphy was appointed to the Health IT Standards Committee, a federal advisory body to the Office of the National Coordinator for Health Information Technology, established by the American Recovery and Reinvestment Act of 2009.

Miriam Paramore, FHIMSS, is Senior Vice President of Corporate Strategy and Government Services for Emdeon. In this role, she is responsible for long-term strategic planning, thought leadership, public policy, and government affairs. Ms. Paramore brings over 25 years of industry experience and plays a critical role in helping Emdeon shape a course for the future based on emerging trends in health IT. She is a national speaker and currently serves on the Board of Directors for HIMSS, as well as on the Board for CareSource Management Group, a non-profit Medicaid managed care organization. She is a past chair of the HIMSS Financial Systems Steering Committee, and serves on the eHealth Advisory Committee for the Commonwealth of Kentucky. As a longtime advocate for health IT in the public sector, Ms. Paramore serves as an advisor to key Congressional committees and the Congressional Budget Office on health IT, healthcare administrative simplification, and other practical solutions that can take costs out of the system and make healthcare more efficient.

David W. Roberts, MPA, FHIMSS, is Vice President of Government Relations for HIMSS. He also serves as Senior Executive for the HIMSS Virginia Office, which includes the Office of Advocacy and Public Policy. Prior to joining HIMSS in August 2002, Mr. Roberts served as a corporate officer for a Fortune 500 company where he focused on health IT. Previous service includes serving as a financial analyst for the U.S. Air Force in the Pentagon and Germany. He has served as a staff assistant to U.S. Sen. Lowell Weicker Jr. (R-Conn.), on the U.S. Senate Subcommittee on the Handicapped, and as a senior professional staff member on the U.S. House Appropriations Committee. In addition, Mr. Roberts has worked on three U.S. presidential campaigns and as a staff assistant for Virginia State Sen. Patsy Ticer (D-Alexandria) in the Virginia General Assembly. In 2008, Mr. Roberts received a two-year federal appointment to the national Advisory Panel on Medicare Education. Also, in 2008, he served as a founding member of the National Collaboration for Health IT for the Underserved and was appointed chair of the Collaborative's Policy Workgroup. Mr. Roberts was elected to a four-year term as a member of the Solana Beach (Calif.) City Council in 2004, appointed Mayor in 2008, and began serving a second four-year term in 2008.

K. Meredith Taylor, MPH, serves as Director of Congressional Affairs for HIMSS. In this role, Ms. Taylor leads HIMSS' public policy activities on Capitol Hill. Prior to serving in this role, she served as HIMSS' Manager of State Government Relations, where she was responsible for maximizing HIMSS' grassroots advocacy activities. Prior to joining HIMSS, she served as Senior Policy Analyst at the National Governors Association (NGA). In this role, she directed the activities of the State Alliance for e-Health's Health Care Practice and Health Information Communication and Data Exchange Taskforces and spearheaded the NGA's policies on public health informatics and telehealth. Ms. Taylor also served as professional staff for U.S. Sen. Thomas R. Carper on the U.S. Senate Committee on Homeland Security and Governmental Affairs' Subcommittee on Federal Financial Management, Government Information and International Security. As professional staff, she was responsible for supporting Sen. Carper's legislative activities pertaining to electronic government. She arranged Congressional oversight hearings on the federal government's IT projects and also developed legislation concerning electronic personal health records and the Federal Employees Health Benefits Program (FEHBP). Ms. Taylor is devoted to public service. She has volunteered for senate and presidential campaigns and is also a member of the Alexandria Public Health Advisory Commission in Alexandria, Virginia.

Dedication

This book is dedicated to anyone who has ever been or will be a patient of the healthcare system. Every day, I try and find a way to make a difference for each of you.

Acknowledgments

I want to acknowledge those people who have made a difference and enabled the development of this text:

My wife, Michelle, and our children Ben, Graham, Nathan, and Christine, have all been encouraging of this work and have given of their time with me in order for this work to be delivered. It is time they cannot have back. I am thankful and humbled by their sacrifices.

My chapter authors and the staff of the HIMSS preconference workshop "Introduction to Healthcare and IT Enabling Technologies" have been pivotal in inspiring the creation of this text. Their knowledge and experience bring a depth and breadth of understanding that makes *Introduction to Healthcare Information Enabling Technologies* unique.

Finally, I would like to acknowledge the publisher, HIMSS, and the Publications Department staff, for their patience and encouragement in bringing this book to life.

Thank you!

Table of Contents

Foreword by David F. Durenberger xv

Preface xvii

Introduction xix

Chapter 1. Musings of a CIO 1
George T. (Buddy) Hickman, FHIMSS, CPHIMS

**Chapter 2. An Overview of the U.S. Health System and Public
Policy Implications** 19
David W. Roberts, MPA, FHIMSS, and K. Meredith Taylor, MPH

Chapter 3. Challenges Facing Hospitals: Perspectives of the CFO 31
Raymond A. Gensinger, Jr., MD, CPHIMS, FHIMSS,
and Larry Kryzaniak, FHFMA

Chapter 4. Follow the Money: The Revenue Cycle Story 43
Miriam Paramore, FHIMSS

Chapter 5. Physicians' Views on Clinical Information Technology 57
Raymond A. Gensinger, Jr., MD, CPHIMS, FHIMSS

Chapter 6. Nursing Informatics and IT-Enabling Technologies 71
Donna B. DuLong, BSN, RN, and Judy Murphy, RN, FACMI, FHIMSS

Chapter 7. Lessons Learned from IT-Enabled Clinical Transformation 87
Melinda Yates Costin and Marion J. Ball, EdD, FACMI, FCHIME, FHIMSS, FAAN

**Chapter 8. How Are We Doing in the Health IT Industry? What's Working?
What's Not?** 95
Kent L. Gale

**Chapter 9. Wrapping It Up: The CEO Perspective on Technologies
in Healthcare** 115
T. Douglas Lawson

Acronyms Used in this Book 121

Index 125

Foreword

The election of a Republican to the U.S. Senate seat Ted Kennedy held in Massachusetts was only one in a series of events which indicate how challenging change is in what passes for the American healthcare system. Everything about President Obama's efforts at health policy reform has led one to believe it is a near impossible task. Well, it is and it isn't.

I began a career, which included three terms in the U.S. Senate as a Republican, on the Senate's Finance Committee and HELP Committee, as a Minnesota business and professional person interested in what we could do to contain healthcare cost increases. I learned quickly the importance of information in improving healthcare choices, quality, accessibility, and affordability. From the time I arrived in the Senate in 1978, I also learned how important good information is to making good policy decisions—just as it is recognized how necessary it is for physicians to make good decisions and to facilitate patient decision-making.

Dr. Atul Gawande, the pediatric oncology surgeon at Brigham & Women's Hospital and Children's Hospital, both in Boston, suggests in his latest book The Checklist Manifesto, that America has invested so much in developing new information to bridge the knowledge gaps in medicine that professionals can no longer get enough training or sub-specialization to know everything he or she needs to know. As a result, we become more aware of the accidental illness and death that occurs because of hospitalizations and surgery. That's where systems come in. That's where health information systems have their greatest promise. Miriam Paramore puts it best on page 55: "We revere the medical industry for developing new and seemingly miraculous advances in diagnostic technologies on a regular basis. How can the industry that saves lives, develops ways to heal, and discovers cures, lag behind in (information) technology?" This occurs in part because the policy-making industry lacks evidence of high value healthcare that comes only with good information systems.

Health reform is a journey, not a destination. President Obama may well sign policy reform legislation. He has already committed billions of dollars to enhance investment in health information technology. As we learned once again in the past months, policy-makers suffer to a degree from too little information and too much ideology. It is imperative that the professionals they represent in healthcare provide them with the lessons they need about what should be paid for and how investment priorities need be made.

Introduction to Healthcare Information Enabling Technologies is an essential read for everyone interested in health system reform and in the role the right information, in the hands of the right people, at the right time, and for the right purpose must play in health system reform. There are lots of books out on what's wrong with the system. This one informs us on what we can do to change it.

David F. Durenberger
U.S. Senator (R-MN 1978–95)
Chair, National Institute of Health Policy
Senior Health Policy Fellow, University of St. Thomas, MN

Preface

I sit here and look at my bookshelf in the office and then later tonight will do the same to the bookcase in my home office. On those shelves are a myriad of textbooks of medicine, business, leadership, and management. These are four very different professions that I do my best to stay on top of year after year, as my career has evolved from the role of medical student in a primary care focused medical school to my current role as chief medical information officer for Fairview Health Services in Minneapolis. Appearing from the top of each book are well-weathered and dog-eared self stick notes suggesting there is something of value on the pages to which they are affixed. Each serves as a reference at times when I need to communicate with others regarding the importance of medical information technology. I am sure that each of my fellow authors and contributors has done the same.

This book, *Introduction to Healthcare Information Enabling Technologies*, is the result of a highly successful preconference workshop that has been presented at the Healthcare Information and Management Systems Society (HIMSS) annual meeting starting in 2008. The contributors and I felt that there were sufficient texts to share with those within healthcare–the nuances of how to be a better leader, run a better business, or perhaps even how to be a better clinician. We noted, however, that there really was a void in the space representing how to get started in healthcare and information technology, especially if you were coming into this field lacking a healthcare background. The twist for this text is in the perspective from which it is written.

This book is meant to help you, the reader, gain the perspective of how we, as organizational leaders, depend on the IT infrastructure to make our organizations, and healthcare in general, a better business. The book is intended for students, professionals entering healthcare, legislators beginning to understand the depth of the healthcare industry and even consumers who are trying to understand the nuance and complexity of the industry of medicine. We will share with you how we connect with health IT as both the consumer of the product and the leaders of the organizations responsible for its successful creation and utilization.

The introduction is meant to be the highest level of overview of health IT. It will cover most of the enabling technologies that are currently in use within healthcare, in addition to the external influences on the healthcare industry that are responsible for the industries' need for rapid change. There are many texts that can take you more deeply into the specifics of health IT. Many of those have been referenced throughout the chapters and would serve as good specific references in the reader's library.

In addition to several perspectives from organizational "chiefs," included are chapters that offer the legislative, revenue cycle, and industry evaluation perspectives. These are meant to complement and complete the understanding of the industry overview to ensure that you have the opportunity to see the complete picture.

You will find that the chapters change voice from one to the next. I have purposefully allowed each of the contributors the latitude to uniquely emphasize those aspects of the healthcare industry. We each see the technologies very differently, and it is important to reflect that. You will see that several of the contributors look at healthcare technologies very personally and others address it in a very businesslike manner. I believe those voice differences are very important in understanding the relationship of the role and the technologies themselves as to how they impact our day-to-day work. I have asked the contributors to try and use specific examples from their experiences to help the reader understand more clearly. To create that emphasis, there will be reference to some vendors and their experiences with those vendors. This text is not intended to provide vendor evaluations. Over time, those vendors that have been working in this space for a long time have had periods of exemplary performance, as well as times of considerable challenge. Often, the experiences related have more to do with timing and our relationships with the vendors, more than the overall vendor's long term performance in the marketplace. This text is not intended to provide vendor evaluations.

We hope you find this text to be both an easy read and a useful tool in your introduction to healthcare. The size and complexity of the industry make it very easy to become compartmentalized within an individual silo of the system and lose sight of the overall goal of the industry: we are trying to provide the safest and highest quality healthcare for all.

Raymond A. Gensinger, Jr., MD, CPHIMS, FHIMSS

Introduction

By Raymond A. Gensinger, Jr., MD, CPHIMS, FHIMSS

The umbrella term *healthcare-enabling technologies* describes the assortment of computational tools and processes that continue to evolve and mature for the betterment of patient care and the ability to manage the business of caring for patients. Healthcare in the United States can be viewed as one of the most inventive and pioneering systems in the world. University medical centers and many other large healthcare systems are the destinations of medical tourists seeking the most advanced services the world can provide. Today, many of these same systems have begun to export their knowledge and services to new locations in Europe, the Middle East and Asia.

In this introduction, we will cover a very high-level overview of many of the technologies and processes that have advanced the U.S. healthcare engine to the place that it is today. We will also introduce many of the external influences that originate from both the public and private sector locations that are responsible for some of the innovations we will discuss in this book. Many of these points of review will be highlighted and referenced in the chapters that follow.

PREPARATION AND ADAPTATION

Caring for each other is an element of human behavior. The development of a healthcare system is a natural evolution of the caring nature of humans. This legacy is founded on attention and physical contact between the ill and their caregivers. Over time, we have added infrastructure to make care provision more efficient and to serve public health needs. The change, however, has been fairly incremental, slow, and evolutionary. For years, the education of medical professionals was accomplished through mentorships and apprenticeships. The first medical schools began in the 16th and 17th centuries, with nursing schools not being founded until late into the 19th century.

Legacy and tradition have deep roots that can be difficult to alter. The advent of Medicare in 1965 ushered in a new opportunity, as more reimbursement was available to support the development of more aggressive end-of-life interventions in the treatment of cardiovascular diseases and chronic renal diseases. Most clinicians adapted quickly and energetically to new diagnostic and therapeutic opportunities in that they would provide better patient outcomes. As the managed care movement of the 1990s took hold, so did a great external influence on the medical profession. The Joint Commission (formerly known as The Joint Commission on Accreditation of Healthcare Organizations or JCAHO) began having a stronger influence on the process of healthcare within hospitals. By late 1999, the publication of the Institute of Medicine's seminal report *To Err is Human: Building a Safer Health System*[1] brought focus onto a healthcare system that lacked focus and tools to safely and consistently care for its patients.

The attention raised by the publication's reporting of 44,000 to 98,000 hospitalized patients dying unnecessarily each year was a wake up call for the industry.[1] Unfortunately, tradition or culture was not easy to change within the healthcare system. Although it was not difficult to begin to identify the types of enabling technologies that were needed by those providing care to improve the environment, the challenge became how to embed the new processes and technologies within the current environments without creating greater havoc than they were intended to resolve. Additionally, these new enabling technologies were coming with steep price tags at the same time reimbursement to both large institutions and individual providers was being reduced. Hospitals had to begin to make choices between obtaining MRI scanners, building new facilities, or implementing advanced medical record keeping systems. Providers had to accept the fact there really was not much "art" left in the practice of medicine. Now was the time to embrace the evidence supporting the use of enabling technologies and incorporate these technologies into their medical practices on a daily basis.

HEALTHCARE REGULATION

CMS

The outside influences on medicine have been growing since the mid 1960s. At first, the Medicare program was a tremendous opportunity in that it provided medical insurance to the nation's elderly population. With the availability of a payment source, many new technologies addressing the needs of this specific population began to be developed. Advanced cardiovascular care through medical and interventional cardiology supported the development of cardiac catheterization laboratories, cardiovascular imaging, balloon, and eventually, stent-based angioplasty. Over time, the Centers for Medicare & Medicaid Services (CMS) became more of a cost-controlling organization, particularly in response to rising hospital and physician fees throughout the 1980s. Eventually Medicare fee schedules limited what physicians were able to bill Medicare beneficiaries for above and beyond the Medicare payment itself. This, along with tight control on diagnosis related group (DRG) payments to hospitals, began to "pinch" finances for health systems.

HIPAA

In 1996, Congress passed the Health Insurance Portability and Accountability Act (HIPAA). Administered by CMS, this legislation facilitates an individual's ability to maintain insurance when changing jobs. The larger impact of HIPAA, however, came in its administrative simplification provisions, which required the development and utilization of standard transaction sets and the privacy and protection of patient medical data during transmission. Standard transaction sets were a leap forward for the business office functions and fostered advancement in the revenue cycle segment of enabling technologies; however, the privacy standards of HIPAA became a surprising and unexpected hurdle for many organizations to accept. While few could argue with the intent, the processes necessary for the successful implementation of these regulations really began to stretch organizations' capabilities to track and monitor data at the same time business was becoming more automated. For some hospitals, these two elements of the HIPAA legislation, plus greater auditing and oversight by CMS, resulted in the creation of corporate compliance departments responsible for identifying erroneous utilization of data and billing irregularities.

The Joint Commission

The Joint Commission was established in 1951 to facilitate the voluntary accreditation of hospitals. This organization has continued to evolve its accreditation standards in addition to its actual method of hospital accreditation. Hospitals are now responsible for measuring themselves against a very long list of standards and regularly reporting those results back to The Joint Commission. This evolution has also had an effect on the healthcare system. Efforts by The Joint Commission and CMS to track ongoing core measures of quality have influenced healthcare organizations' needs for more clinical data tools, and processes for capturing, measuring compliance, and reporting results against the defined core measures. The current evidence-based core measure set is listed in Table 1.

Table 1: Current Evidence-Based Core Measure Set

Acute Myocardial Infarction AMI	Children's Asthma Care CAC
Heart Failure HF	Surgical Care Improvement Project SCIP
Pneumonia PN	Hospital Outpatient Measures HOP
Pregnancy and Related Conditions PR	Venous Thromboembolism VTE
Hospital-Based Inpatient Psychiatric Services HBIPS	Stroke STK

ONC

In 2004, the Office of the National Coordinator for Health Information Technology (ONC) was created within the U.S. Department of Health and Human Services (HHS) by executive order of then President George W. Bush. ONC is responsible for counseling the HHS secretary and providing leadership for the development of an interoperable health IT infrastructure. This office has recently had significant growth and impact with funds that have become available through the American Recovery and Reinvestment Act of 2009 (ARRA); the health IT provisions of ARRA go under the acronym "HITECH," which stands for Health Information Technology for Economic and Clinical Health Act of 2009.

CCHIT

Founded in 2004, the Certification Commission for Health Information Technology (CCHIT) is a not-for-profit organization committed to advancing the adoption of health IT. The organization spent the first two years developing the criteria by which electronic health record (EHR) systems would be measured and certified; the first products were certified by CCHIT in 2006. Certification adds credibility to vendors and to the products they are bringing to the market while, at the same time, provides the consumer, hospital, or clinic with a level of comfort that the vendors they are selecting have at least made a commitment to developing products designed to improve healthcare delivery. To date, CCHIT has been the only pathway for certification for EHR vendors. The ARRA legislation continues to recognize CCHIT as a certification body but has opened the door for vendors to achieve certification via alternative, yet to be determined pathways.

ARRA

ARRA was created in response to declining economic conditions in the United States. While the entire act created funds of close to $800 billion, only $147 billion went to healthcare. Of those funds, $19 billion was earmarked for health IT. These funds are being invested in healthcare to create interoperable electronic medical record systems for both individual healthcare providers and hospitals. The "catch" to these funds is the expectation that utilizing these electronic systems will result in the meaningful use of such technologies. On December 30, 2009, HHS released the Notice of Proposed Rule Making establishing the Electronic Health Record Incentive Program, better known as 'meaningful use,' and the Interim Final Rule establishing the Initial Set of Standards, Implementation Specifications and Certification Criteria for EHR Technology.[2] Each rule now has a public comment period followed by an internal review and edit.

Information on both rules is available on the CMS Web site (http://www.cms. hhs.gov/recovery/11_healthit.asp).[2] Additional analysis on both rules is available on the Healthcare Information and Management Systems Society (HIMSS) Web site at www.himss.org/meaningfuluse (some content is exclusive to HIMSS' members).

As of this writing in early 2010, it is expected that final rules will be published in late spring 2010. These final rules are the legal guidance all must follow to be eligible for the Medicare and Medicaid EHR Incentive Programs.

An important part of the meaningful use criteria is the expectation of interoperability between healthcare providers. Again, the full expectation of interoperability is not yet determined but will play a pivotal role in one's success in meeting meaningful use criteria. If the definition is limited to a certain percentage of patient interactions or can be satisfied by the movement of patients within one's own healthcare system, it is likely many organizations will be successful. If the definition requires complete exchange between any two providers, regardless of system, then there is going to be a huge enabling technology gap waiting to be filled.

HITECH

The HITECH component of ARRA legislation provides for $44,000 to $65,000 per provider for the meaningful use of EHRs as an incentive for the rapid adoption of IT.

In addition to the provider incentives, there are funds for the development of health information organizations responsible for creating a data exchange infrastructure and for regional extension centers. Regional extension centers will offer technical assistance, education, guidance, and best practice information to accelerate the adoption of health IT.

Healthcare systems and providers are on the edge of a vast chasm. We are being offered funds, support, and guidance in the adoption of IT to help us move from the methods of healthcare we are currently operating in to the computerized healthcare environment of the future. To achieve that bridge, we have to adopt a series of existing technologies and assist in developing the next generation of enabling healthcare IT.

CURRENT ENABLING DEPARTMENTAL SYSTEMS

A typical healthcare system today is made up of hundreds, if not thousands, of stand-alone applications in support of the overall business. In healthcare, there are often three or four distinct areas of IT. Those technologies can be grouped into financial or business office systems, clinical systems, infrastructure, or networks; depending on the organization, bioelectronics may be considered yet another technology area. Many of these technologies are single purpose and "disconnected" from many of the organization's other systems. While each may be a "best-of-breed" for the service it delivers, many organizations are finding they have sacrificed the value of systems that effectively connect with one another in favor of systems that best serve only the few making use of the applications. We will examine some of the more visible applications across the healthcare continuum.

Registration and Scheduling

The front door of a clinic or hospital system is often the business office or registration portal. Registration and scheduling systems are often linked to a single vendor in support of the organization's centralized services. This ensures patients are accurately identified and entered into the organization's system. The processes also establish the relationships between the patient and the necessary providers of care and identify individuals who have responsibility for the billing aspects of these encounters. Uniquely identifying an individual and the relationships between family members, as well as distinctions between those patients with identical names, is a critical step within the registration process. As organizations become more automated, failure to uniquely identify a patient could result in merging medical information for completely unrelated individuals. Alternately, if a patient registration is not correctly tied to the same previously registered patient, duplication of patient records is the result. In those situations, the results and activities of care are tied to the unique encounters within which results are generated. If the providers are unaware of duplicate medical records, they will not look for additional information "housed" in different accounts.

Financial Applications

After registration and scheduling, the systems responsible for managing the financial aspects of a patient-healthcare provider encounter are often referred to as revenue cycle systems. These applications may be the same as the registration and scheduling applications, but not necessarily. Revenue cycle systems have responsibility for managing accounts internally but also often have to provide the "bridges" to the outside world of healthcare payers. Revenue cycle systems "reach out" and preauthorize payment for activities based on coverage and indications, as well as manage billing and adjudication of claims following medical care. The complexity of the transaction requires frequent human intervention, so an important component of the effectiveness of a revenue cycle system is how well it can organize and generate meaningful work queues for billing office staff to manage. As the revenue cycle is the life blood of a healthcare organization, the time between a provision of service and a return of funds to cover the costs of that care is critical. The longer the interval between service and payment, the less efficient the organization is and the greater the risk of no payment at all.

Medical Laboratory and Radiology Departments

Outside of the business offices of a healthcare system, the most likely place to find enabling technologies are the medical laboratory and radiology departments. Many laboratories are not "new" to enabling technologies, having utilized such technologies for an extended period of time and having to comply with special certification requirements through the Clinical Laboratory Improvement Amendment (CLIA). The laboratory has many individual devices for performing specific tests, but the central laboratory system is responsible for gathering and organizing those data. In radiology, there is a division of labor between the radiology information system (RIS) and the picture archiving and communication system (PACS). The procedures are scheduled and protocoled within the RIS, the imaging is captured within the individual digital modalities (CT, MRI, mammography, ultrasound, etc.), and the digital output is forwarded and stored within the PACS. While not every organization has full digital workflows within the radiology department, this is becoming more common than not. Early development and adoption of the Digital Imaging and Communications in Medicine (DICOM) standards has made it easier for organizations to digitize radiology. These standards have improved the ease with which images can move across the Internet to wherever the radiologist is located or wherever the patient will next receive care.

Cardiovascular Care

An area of emerging IT is within the cardiovascular suite. The cardiovascular information system (CVIS) is responsible for the scheduling, protocols, and documentation of the procedures within the cardiovascular department. Many vendors are currently supplying cardiovascular specific imaging archives that mirror a PACS, but this is an inefficient storage strategy. As PACS are maturing and data storage is moving to network attached storage strategies, it is possible to merge the imaging of multiple varying modalities into a single multimodal PACS solution. The uniqueness the CVIS adds to the environment is the complex documentation of the procedures themselves. The cardiovascular suite integrates waveforms, electrical impulses and rhythms, and direct pressure measurements during the procedures. Many of these are far more complex than documentation within the radiology suite.

A Hospital System's Workflow-driven Areas

Operating Room. As we move away from the departmental modalities of laboratory, radiology, and cardiology, we move into the workflow-driven areas of the hospital systems. Within the operating room (OR), there are many opportunities to utilize enabling technologies, such as tracking equipment, tissues, and devices going from the equipment tray to the patient and vice versa. An OR's effectiveness comes from choreographing the multiple providers of care, patients, rooms, and the constant associated interventions. As a featured revenue center for a healthcare system, inefficiency in this space can quickly have significant negative financial impact on an organization. In the OR, there is opportunity for bar coding and radio frequency identification (RFID) to facilitate processes. This is in addition to technologies that assist in managing the anesthetic portions of a procedure. The workflow in this space is the focus, thus, patient- and provider-tracking technologies are prominently used in the OR. Often represented on very large grease boards or electronic tracking boards, the central scheduling area serves as the "air traffic control" point for all of the OR.

The complexity and specificity of the work in the OR made it an early site for enabling technology in a hospital. Often that was made at the expense of interconnectivity with other hospital systems. On a good day, the scheduling and registration of the OR was connected with other hospital systems, but that was not a guarantee. Many times the value of the system within the OR made the need for duplicate data entry or reentry of information a necessary component of the work. Today, with core measures focused on surgical interventions, it is becoming more important that the surgery and hospital information systems become more tightly interoperable than they have been historically. This is an emerging area of opportunity for healthcare information technologies.

Emergency Department. In many ways, the emergency department (ED) can be viewed as very similar to the OR. The activities here rely more upon the flow of patients, providers, and information in and out of the ED than on any particular technology in and of itself. Once again, the grease board or electronic tracking board is the central feature that differentiates an efficient ED from an inefficient ED. The difference between the ED and the OR has to do with the unexpected complexity of the care provided. The OR can plan for the day, while the ED is at the whim of the weather and "cycles of the moon." Clear documentation of the patient's story as he or she passes from provider to provider along the critical care path can mean the difference between good and bad outcomes of care. Additionally, the ability to acquire a patient's medical history at the onset of an encounter and then, later, at the end of the encounter, to transmit the summary of care out of the ED, is the foundation for effective transition of care between the ED and other departments within the hospital.

ELECTRONIC HEALTH RECORDS

An EHR can be described as the sum total of clinical applications that, at the very least, is responsible for aggregating patient-related data and presenting that information in an organized and cohesive way back to individuals providing patient care. This was the legacy for many "homegrown" electronic *medical* records (EMR) and data repositories that have since been replaced by more fully functional and integrated electronic *health* records (EHRs). Definitions vary but the distinctions between a medical record and a health record can be differentiated in that the medical records are often representative of fairly limited elements of care and focus on treatment of a single organization, usually in the acute care environment, while a health record has a much broader context involving multiple encounters and providers, both inpatient and outpatient, and has tools or evidence-based alerts and reminders that assist in managing the patient's health or well-being, rather than individual disease events. According to the organization previously known as the National Alliance for Health Information Technology (NAHIT–note that NAHIT ceased operations in August 2009, citing completion of its mission to raise the awareness of health IT), the distinctions are as follows:[3]

EMR: The electronic record of health-related information on an individual that is created, gathered, managed, and consulted by licensed clinicians and staff from a single organization who are involved in the individual's health and care.

EHR: The aggregate electronic record of health-related information on an individual that is created and gathered cumulatively across more than one healthcare organization and is managed and consulted by licensed clinicians and staff involved in the individual's health and care.

An EHR application can be made up of a series of applications often available individually or as a bundle. Elements of an EHR include billing, registration, revenue cycle, laboratory, radiology, cardiology, and ED applications—all having documentation tools, and computerized practitioner order entry (CPOE), a clinical data repository, health information management, medication reconciliation, and elements of clinical decision support. Elements of an EHR can be purchased from a number of different vendors, individually in a best-of-breed strategy or, more commonly, as a best-of-cluster or core vendor strategy in which a majority of applications are supplied to the healthcare organization by a single vendor.

The consumer equivalent of the EHR has been identified as the personal health record (PHR). NAHIT has defined the PHR as follows[3]:

PHR: An electronic record of health-related information on an individual that conforms to nationally recognized interoperability standards and that can be drawn from multiple sources while being managed, shared, and controlled by the individual.

As healthcare organizations and EHR vendors have struggled to develop interoperable functionalities to effectively transfer information between organizations in a meaningful way, the notion of the PHR has gained popularity. With the control in the hands of the individual, a concern over the management of and disclosure of private information has been transferred to the individual for management. This does not take organizations and vendors "off the hook," but gives them an option of transferring data to the patient's control rather than directly communicating with each other. Interoperability requirements within ARRA are likely to facilitate the transfer of data to and from PHRs, as well as facilitate the necessity of EHRs to effectively communicate.

PHR effectiveness and adoption rates are going to be watched with intrigue by both healthcare systems and vendors. Patients currently manage their medical information with wide degrees of attention. Many patients have little or no understanding of their medical conditions and medications—some out of ignorance, while others lack the intellectual capability altogether. Others still, have limited or no access to the computing services necessary to leverage a PHR. PHRs will likely have growing value for individuals as the market segment matures. However, immediately, they have value for individuals with personal chronic illness or who are responsible for a parent or child with chronic medical conditions requiring multiple care providers. The benefits of organizing and carrying health information in a key fob or having it as close as a Web browser have yet to be fully documented or realized.

ENABLING SYSTEMS CAPABILITIES

Once a departmental or organizational technology is put in place, it opens up the possibility for additional functionalities to be added to existing applications to extend their capabilities. The establishment of CPOE as a standalone system or as part of an EHR now presents an opportunity to begin directly transmitting prescription information to the pharmacy. Starting in 2009, CMS began paying a bonus to organizations utilizing e-prescribing for greater than 50% of its Medicare patient visits. After several years' time, organizations that have not yet initiated e-prescribing will see a reduction in their reimbursements coming from CMS. The financial incentives are in place to encourage the early adoption of technologies that greatly reduce the risk of transcription errors and the likelihood of fraudulent prescriptions.

SSO Function and Context Management Systems

Where e-prescribing is considered an add-on function to an EHR system, there are other enabling technologies that can be placed in front of the system to assist providers. The most visible forms of an enabling technology in front of EHR systems are the single sign on (SSO) function and context management systems. SSO tools, which work at the level of the workstation desktop, register a single set of credentials and pass that knowledge on to all appropriate applications for which the user has access. This simplifies the login process for a provider. Prior to SSO, providers in our organization had to remember as many as 13 passwords to take advantage of our clinical technologies. SSO cannot necessarily cover all applications, but it can manage many of the most commonly used applications, saving providers time and creating more secure environments. The environment is more secure because there is less temptation for individuals to write down their passwords or to use easy to remember passwords that could potentially be compromised.

A complementary technology to SSO is known as *context management*. The technology is referred to as the clinical context object workgroup or CCOW. CCOW-enabled applications have the capacity to pass patient level contextual information from one application to the next. When partnered with SSO, providers can easily move between one application and the next without needing to log in or find the same patient and encounter in subsequently accessed applications. This is an effective, comprehensive solution for organizations that have not moved to a core vendor strategy or even for organizations that have a core vendor but also other significant clinical applications. It is an efficient solution; however, it lacks the elegance of applications that house multiple data types in a single system. The integrated data offer more analytic opportunities that can be completed "on the fly."

Bioelectronics Enabling Technologies

The department of bioelectronics is one of growing importance to a healthcare organization. In the past, the department was responsible for moving around the initial electronics devices, such as monitoring equipment, ventilators, and other centrally-supplied devices. They had responsibility for managing effective inventory of such equipment and its distribution and maintenance according to manufactured standards, as well as bringing technologies to the bedside. As IT services moved out of the mainframe and data center to deliver networks and PCs to the desktop, the distinction of services began to blur somewhat. Today, when so many patient care devices have the capacity to deliver data to an EHR and require network connectivity to maintain their bios and firmware updates, the distinction between IT and bioelectronics has blurred even further still.

Bioelectronics still tends to have responsibility for devices directly connected to patients for monitoring and therapeutic purposes. Vital signs monitors, the mainstay of the bioelectronics group, have advanced beyond the capacity to track blood pressure, heart rate, and respiration. They can now track O_2 saturation, CO_2 concentration, temperature, and any number of intravascular pressure readings, including cardiac output measurements. Typically, these are hardwired into the network and can connect to the EHR via intermediary technologies supported by IT. Typically, these devices are physically located within the room and have little capacity to move with the patients.

Ventilators and smart pumps are representative of older and newer bioelectronics devices that tend to stay with the patient as he or she traverses the healthcare system. Ventilators are becoming more sophisticated and intelligent. Like the vital signs monitors, they have the capacity to connect to the EHR via a bridging interface. Because of the calibration necessity of this device, it is more closely aligned with historic bioelectronics.

Smart pumps sit very much on the cusp between bioelectronics and IT. Twenty years ago, many intravenous infusions were managed by manually titrating drip rates of the various fluids. Electronic pumps started appearing about 25 years ago and were little more than sophisticated drip calculators. Equipped with sensors to detect obstruction and completion of therapies, they were able to ensure a regular rate of infusion. Since 2008, the next generation of "smart" pumps has begun to appear in hospitals. These pumps not only count drips, they contain customized libraries of the medications to be administered intravenously to ensure that the nurse cannot inadvertently administer a medication at the wrong rate and, therefore, the wrong dose. These have been designed as safety features in medication administration.

Because the pumps are so smart, they are regulated by the U.S. Food and Drug Administration (FDA) and require connectivity to a medication library server. This connectivity not only assures proper medication library information is transmitted to the pumps but also has the ability to track the alarms and errors that are detected in the pump itself. The need for network support, data center services, and analytics monitoring have all shifted smart pump management closer to a true IT function. The need to maintain the devices themselves so they consistently meet manufacturer and FDA standards is still the expertise of the bioelectronics service area.

The convergence of information technologies and bioelectronics is an inevitable expectation organizations must consider preparing for. Some organizations have begun to move bioelectronics services' oversight from the materials management department to the direction of the organization's CIO. This logical reorganization ensures there is a common set of service expectations and harmony when deploying bioelectronic devices, from acquisition, delivery and storage to maintenance.

Dispensing Devices

Outside of the services of bioelectronics and IT, other enabling technologies exist that are overseen or maintained by the pharmacy department and supply chain. The pharmacy department is often responsible for the acquisition, maintenance, and general upkeep of the medication cabinets most hospitals have within their patient care units. Typically connecting to the pharmacy system via the network, these cabinets manage pharmaceutical inventories once they are delivered "out of the hand" of the pharmacy department. The cabinets typically have two kinds of drawers. One set of drawers contains the commonly prescribed medications such as analgesics, acetaminophen, or ibuprofen. The other drawers—patient-specific, contain the appropriate medication prescribed for the patient and dispensed by the pharmacy. These devices can assure the medications are only accessible by those medical staff on the floor with privileges to handle medications and track the coincidence of prescribed-to-obtained times for medications. Some hospitals have begun using a medication administration robot capable of accompanying nursing staff into patient rooms prior to the distribution of medications.

Similar to medication carts, supply stations are giant vending machines containing all of the common disposable commodities used in the day-to-day care of patients. These do not necessarily add to patient safety, but they can track who is removing supplies and in what quantities. The true advantage of these devices is their ability to:
- track floor stock inventories and automatically communicate back to the central supply area so the floor can be restocked.
- automatically pass reorder information to the hospital supplier, eliminating the risk of running out of necessary supplies.

End-User Technologies

Enterprise-wide tools and equipment have been effectively enabling organizations from a corporate management and patient safety perspective over the last two decades. It is important to note that a number of enabling technologies have had their most dramatic effect directly upon the organization's end-users. Clearly, the addition of PCs and workstations distributed throughout the healthcare system has had a dramatic impact on the ease and speed of communication of orders, results, and medical knowledge. Today, many organizations are challenged by the ability to deliver even more computers into the workspace to support the needs of so many organizational end users. The construction of our latest children's hospital is being designed to accommodate up to four computers per single patient room: one PC for the patient, one for the provider, and one for family members, all located directly within the patient room. The fourth PC is located immediately outside each patient room. The PC outside the room was important so staff members can monitor the patient from afar and continue their documentation.

The addition of wireless networking into the infrastructure of a healthcare environment allowed for a newfound degree of flexibility and autonomy that had been lacking in the wired world. Workstations can now be located nearly anywhere without needing network wiring. Battery-powered workstations can be located anywhere. Not only do employees have greater flexibility, the patient can, too. More monitoring devices can piggyback off the wireless network, allowing the patient more freedom of ambulation during his or her inpatient stay. Wireless technology has also benefitted family members, who are able to have guest access to an Internet connection without needing any more equipment than their wireless-enabled laptop or handheld device.

Once the wireless network infrastructure was in place, manufacturers became more creative in the design and function of the devices developed for the healthcare environment. Table PCs and personal digital assistants (PDAs) offered two new devices that were mobile <u>and</u> attached to the network. No longer tethered to the locations where PCs were placed, staff could complete work while on the move throughout the workspace.

Unfortunately, the tablet PCs and PDAs suffered from small screen real estate, short battery life, and less functionality than their larger PC counterparts. The computer on wheels (COW), also known as the workstation on wheels (WOW), was born. These devices were either fully functional PCs loaded onto special carts with heavy-duty battery supplies or high-end laptop computers. The first generations of these devices offered little flexibility in ergonomics, were dreadfully heavy, and often had fairly poor battery life, requiring frequent tethering. Some required frequent enough recharges that the staff eventually just parked them in the halls permanently plugged into the nearest electrical receptacle. Today's versions are highly flexible ergonomically, have battery life that can extend 8 to 12 hours and, while still may remain heavy, they have much improved types of wheels and designs to assist in their movement throughout the environment.

More specialized handheld devices such as barcode readers have been introduced to assist in several different areas. These readers can facilitate the positive identification of patients, regardless of their ability to effectively communicate. They have been utilized to support the five rights in medication administration: right patient, right drug, right time, right dose, and right route of administration. In support of these rights, documentation is eased and the opportunities for transcription and translation errors of documentation are effectively eliminated. Additionally, these readers can facilitate the process of sample labeling by providing point-of-care verification of patient and orders, while producing mini barcode labels that can be affixed to each of the sample vials for processing within the laboratory. Sample vials with barcodes can greatly reduce the risk of misidentification of tests performed within the lab.

The number and functionality of end-user technology enabling devices is sure to continue to grow as the business of healthcare continues to move further away from physical "brick and mortar" facilities. Patients will be engaging in more personal healthcare with the addition of mobile blood pressure monitors and smart home equipment that transmits weights and activity levels to monitoring stations. More providers themselves are moving into the community to facilitate patient care, managing care more remotely in support of lower costs and greater patient convenience and independence.

Identification Modalities

Accurate patient identification at the time of registration has already been identified as an important process. When patient identification is done improperly, the risks can have downstream effects. Once the patient is within the hospital, the risks of misidentification can be catastrophic to the patient. The literature and lay press have focused on reports of patient misidentification and the subsequent adverse events that have occurred. There have been improper surgeries, misdosed cancer therapies, and newborn infants sent home with the wrong parents. These true and often sensationalized events represent only the "tip of the iceberg," as there is little discussion of the events that have resulted in little or no harm.

Healthcare is beginning to take a cue from other industries and is exploring and implementing the barcoding of patient identification wristbands in an effort to minimize the risk of patient misidentification. These barcodes can contain several important pieces of information that are literally "on" the patient, including their name and other identifying information, the patient's providers, and allergies. They can also be used to properly link mothers, fathers, and newborn infants. When combined with an EHR's capacity to read these codes and link the identification with the care plans in the record, the opportunity for enhanced safety and quality is markedly raised.

Implementation challenges within healthcare have been the cause of its slow adoption.[4] Success in medication administration is tied to the organizational ability to barcode unit dose medications. When many medications are purchased in bulk and redistributed, unit dosing now becomes the responsibility of the organization to manage. Some organizations have underestimated the costs and the complexities of implementation, while others have been cautious in considering whether auto-ID functions, such as radio frequency identification (RFID), would be a better modality and, therefore, are willing to wait.

RFID technologies offer great promise in healthcare, with functions that can be far superior to barcode technologies and are more likely to be complementary applications than competitive technologies. RFID's capability to "find" equipment, patients, and even missing sponges in the OR is a function far exceeding the functions of a barcode identification system. Unit dose identification of medication, however, continues to be an issue, even with the RFID solutions. Also, current RFID solutions remain expensive, while barcoding solutions have continued to drop in price.

The capacity to store data is greatly enhanced with RFID over barcoding. Additional information that can be maintained might include more detailed manufacturer information or perhaps even segments of medical record information that can be used for patient care in the event of central EHR downtimes, a patient-specific data backup of sorts. The technology has two modes, and its utility may be limited by whether the RFID device is active or passive. An active device is powered with a small battery and is therefore always identifiable in the environment, but the battery must be maintained. A passive device is potentially always available but requires an exciting agent to generate the energy for the device to transmit its information. Once again, there is likely to be an opportunity of both types of RFID modalities to be utilized within a healthcare environment.

Organizations need to start now to develop an identification strategy. The strategy needs to include all three identification modalities: barcoding, active RFID, and passive RFID. As barcoding is reasonably affordable to implement, it is an appropriate technology organizations can begin investing in now while continuing to monitor the RFID space and planning for its implementation, as the business cases warrant.

Health Information Exchanges

The concept of a regional health information exchange (HIE) was born in the late 1980s and early 1990s out of telecom companies' search for new ways to sell circuits between healthcare providers. Also during this time, the first telemedicine programs were developed; these programs "married" the maturing videoconferencing market with newly developed assessment tools, such as remote dermatologic cameras, digital stethoscopes, and digital oto-ophthalmoscopes. This first attempt at inter- and intra-connecting healthcare systems was not very effective on several levels. The circuits themselves were point-to-point or routed through communications hubs and, for competitive organizations, no business advantage was seen in partnering with their competitors. Such partnerships could make it too easy for patients to move in and out of their current healthcare systems and into those of competitors.

At the same time, the Internet was beginning to boom. Over the next decade, communications speed climbed dramatically while the cost of that connectivity dropped. In the early part of the 21st millennium, with the ubiquitous Internet, there was an opportunity for the rebirth of the regional health information networks. During this incarnation, they became referred to as regional health information exchanges (RHIEs) or health information organizations (HIOs). When considered in connection with each other, they make up an infrastructure known as the nationwide health information network (NHIN). As EHR vendors' software became more sophisticated and some required remote hosting, the applications themselves could be run over the Internet. The flexibility and availability of the Internet rekindled the concept of easily moving data from point to point, while ever-improving standards of data definitions, communications protocols, and transmission expectations have all made the concept of data exchange and interoperability a high-priority for healthcare moving into 2010.

An HIE can be structured in many ways, but the two most common architectures are either virtual or physical. In the physical architecture demonstrated in Indiana[5] or Tennessee,[6] data are aggregated in a physical location for availability when appropriate access to that data is requested. In the virtual architecture, only the identifying information necessary to point to organizations that have data is stored centrally. When data are requested, the request is forwarded to the organizations having data and the information is created real-time for presentation. This is the model that can be seen in Minnesota.[7]

In the most current models for development of a health information organization, there is an expectation that the individual exchanges will be responsible for creating interoperability standards for other exchanges that may operate within their state or for any exchanges that operate within adjoining states. This transitive process creates a virtual nationwide information network, provided, of course, that certain key states choose not to create an exchange. The NHIN[8] and its ultimate architecture and standards expectations continue to evolve as of this writing.

Data Warehousing

By bringing all of the enabling technologies together to feed a variety of databases and or clinical data repositories, we are now able to provide analytics far beyond anything that healthcare was ever able to do before. Many organizations would take elements of their data and send them to outside benchmarking organizations. These many organizations would take the data provided from source systems and merge that with additional abstracted data provided by individuals from within the healthcare organization. These data would then be merged with data from yet other organizations into a large analytic database. The data would then be made available via online reports that allow a healthcare organization to compare themselves with other like organizations in the country or perhaps other local organizations that were contributing. The challenges for a healthcare organization were several. First, they often only had limited clinical technologies in place, so that the closest thing they had to clinical diagnostic information was the billing, or International Classification of Diseases version nine (ICD-9) codes. Second, since much of the data needed to still be abstracted from the chart, each organization would need to employ one or more individuals with a responsibility of pulling charts, interpreting and then entering the data into these outside databases. Third, there was never any guarantee that there were going to be suitable compare groups within the database in the future or that, if you chose to change compare groups, the new group would be available. And, finally, once your data was submitted and augmented, there was never a clear guarantee that the data could be returned to you for reanalysis or comparison with other data that may not have been part of the original data sets submitted.

These were the best options available for organizations trying to use analytics and benchmarking to help advance their organizations. Today is different. Most large healthcare organizations now have growing clinical data repositories and thorough financial databases. The combination of these data sources, in addition to more end-user tools for analysis and reporting, has made data warehousing and business analytics reporting within reach of any healthcare organization. In this environment, the missing piece is still the benchmarking data from other organizations.

Elements of data recorded or gathered within the organization move through an evolution of value that can be described as follows:

Data: These are the elemental components of recorded content from any of the systems within any business entity.

Information: As data are brought together, they can be logically organized into recognizable patterns that are acted upon by individuals within the system.

Knowledge: Repeated review and learning from provided information allows the user to begin to reliably predict events and outcomes.

Intelligence: Users are now able to act on the content of information and knowledge to manipulate future events or outcomes.

Wisdom: The value of time and experience that allows the user to know when to accept or reject any of the results determined from the first four levels.

As we move along one axis of data utility and another of time or experience (see Figure 1), we, as users of data, have the opportunity to better understand our patients, our organization, and our business. These analytics driving care and business can be referred to in combination as the organization's *business intelligence* and *data warehousing functions.*

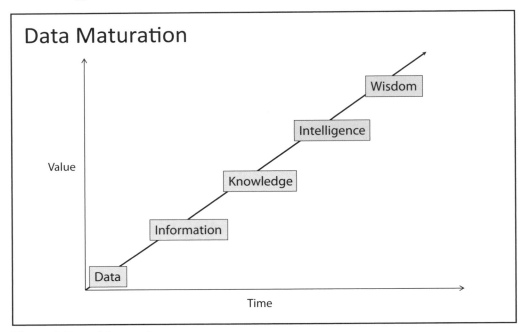

Figure 1: Data Maturation

In today's healthcare environment, we need to be master of our data, for they have multiple opportunities to be repurposed after the specific patient encounter from which they evolved. The data can be repurposed as an aggregate of like populations of patients to demonstrate an organizational competence important in its designation as a "Center of Excellence" for diagnostic and therapeutic purposes. Additionally, when these data are aggregated across different demographic categories, they can be used for the identification of populations for research studies or public health analysis. Regardless of the repurpose, the data have power and value and need to remain within the control of the organization that has generated them.

SUMMARY

The opportunities for new and greater computational tools and healthcare-enabling technologies are endless. Many of the computational tools available today have evolved within the last 20 years, with most within the last 10. Efforts to refine currently available tools and develop newer ones still will only further advance the industry of healthcare. Today, we really are only at the infancy of where we can take our industry. The chapters that follow will take us on a tour of healthcare and healthcare-enabling technologies from the perspective of organizational and national leaders who have tremendous responsibilities. They have responsibility to their patients and their organizations; they have responsibility to healthcare as an industry; and they have responsibility to advance technology as a tool of our industry as well. Each will take you on a tour of healthcare, from their individual perspectives, in an effort to help you fully embrace the breadth of healthcare and information-enabling technologies.

REFERENCES

1. Institute of Medicine. *To Err is Human: Building a Safer Health Care System.* Washington, DC: National Academy Press; 2000.

2. http://www.cms.hhs.gov/recovery/11_healthit.asp. Accessed January 15, 2010.

3. http://nashville.medicalnewsinc.com/news.php?viewStory=1940. Accessed November 12, 2009.

4. Simspon NJ, Kleinberg KA, *Implementation Guide to Bar Coding and Auto-ID in Healthcare, Improving Quality and Patient Safety.* Chicago, Illinois. HIMSS, 2009.

5. http://www.regenstrief.org/medinformatics/inpc. Accessed November 12, 2009.

6. http://www.midsoutheha.org/. Accessed November 12, 2009.

7. http://www.mnhie.org/. Accessed November 12, 2009.

8. http://healthit.hhs.gov/portal/server.pt?open=512&objID=1142&parentname=CommunityPage&parentid=1&mode=2&in_hi_userid=10741&cached=true. Accessed November 14, 2009.

CHAPTER 1

Musings of a CIO

By George T. (Buddy) Hickman, FHIMSS, CPHIMS

INTRODUCTION

There is much that can be said about the chief information officer (CIO) role in healthcare. The role has always had opportunity to shape organizations and the industry, but this statement is truer as never before. Federal government actions present potential for catalyzing health information technology (IT) efforts across our industry, and CIOs are in key positions to provide individual and collective leadership to what may well be a paradigm shift in technology uses in care delivery, health data sharing, and reporting.

The CIO, once integrated into the senior management team and especially if active in the board room, is well-positioned to affect organizational change. While many may view the CIO as the senior technology executive, most CIOs bring many other competencies to bear in serving their organizations and communities.

It is the intent of the musings described herein to provide a window into how the role of the CIO brings value to his or her organization. Further, the expectations of the enterprise leadership may vary with respect to the role, yet the opportunities a CIO can explore in serving that role are most broad, while quite unique relative to other executives' duties.

A QUICK BIT OF HISTORY REGARDING THE ROLE IN HEALTHCARE

The CIO title became popular in the mid/late 1980s. There were many efforts to define this "new role," including efforts to describe what made the CIO different from other IT leaders with the top-ranking titles within their organizations.

Defining the CIO role in healthcare was a similar prospect. The Healthcare Information and Management Systems Society (HIMSS) published a book titled *Guide to Effective Health Care Information and Management Systems and the Role of the Chief*

Information Officer.[1] High-performing CIOs were stated to have the attributes listed in Table 1-1.

Table 1-1: Attributes of High-Performing CIOs[1]

Healthcare Savvy	Flexible	Intelligence, Independence, Influence
Effective and efficient	Empathic to board and community	Results-oriented
Trans-functional skills	Lead by example	Value-add focused
Schmoozers	Technology skills	Deliver early and often
People, process, and leadership focused	Collaborative	Vendor relational
Standard process and procedurally centered		

The guide also provided technical, operational, and management experience requirements for the CIO. These requirements are shown in Table 1-2. The requirements could have minor updates to reflect some changes in industry focus but otherwise still represent some of the key competencies of the CIO.

Table 1-2: Experience Requirements of a CIO[1]

Technical	Operational	Management
Knowledge of systems market	General understanding of all departmental operations	Capable of managing limited resources over multiple projects
Understanding of system installation and support requirements	Knowledge of alternative delivery systems	Able to effectively communicate with management
Awareness of new technologies	Ability to objectively analyze productivity data	Able to analyze financial impact of information systems decisions
General understanding of system capabilities and limitations	Awareness of hospitals' competitive position and factors impacting the market	Capable of developing and implementing a strategic information plan

In 1992, the College of Healthcare Information Management Executives (CHIME) was formed with the dual objective of serving healthcare CIOs' professional development needs and advocating for more effective use of information management within the industry. CHIME grew to more than 250 members during its year of inception, demonstrating that individuals sitting in this role recognized a need to gather for the sake of sharing experiences and knowledge to the benefit of the whole.[2]

There are also naysayers relative to the CIO role that date back to the origin years. *Business Week* published an article entitled, "CIO is Starting to Stand for 'Career is Over'" in early 1990.[3] This phrase has held to the acronym over the years, even being recast as though it is a new phrase by many who encounter it, though a strong majority of my colleagues have well-proved it wrong over the nearly two decades since the suggestion was offered. Nay-saying continues with a more recent suggestion in January 2009 by *Computer World* that "CIOs are Entering a Career Ice Age," playing on the notion that CIOs will follow the course of dinosaurs by "hunkering down" in proverbial tar pits during this time of economic turmoil.[4]

More recently, certification has emerged as a means to demonstrate specific known competencies for the CIO role. CHIME has undertaken an effort to develop a certification process for CIOs. As is the case with other certification examinations, those who obtain the certification will possess the knowledge of the experience and be best positioned to calibrate what competencies are possessed by other certified colleagues.

KEY EXPECTATIONS FOR THE CIO

There are many ways that the CIO role can be described. One author for *CIO* magazine, Christopher Koch, wrote that four archetype CIOs exist:[5]

1. Turnaround artist
2. Operational expert
3. Business leader
4. Innovation agent

Koch posits that *turnaround artist CIOs* bring skills well beyond basic management skills, including extra leadership and change management capabilities. Hence, turnaround CIOs are the most highly compensated.

Operational expert CIOs add value with project management expertise and technology knowledge, positioning IT solution delivery with a far higher degree of leadership agility. Koch states that these CIOs highlight their delivery skills and continue emphasis on delivery to be distinguished beyond other utility players but may face big changes in business alignment and access to resources.

Business leader CIOs have the interpersonal skills and business process knowledge to excel. These CIOs will also emphasize IT governance in how they do their jobs to administer the role and may also look to the next level of management for the hard work of execution.

Finally, *innovation agent CIOs* are those visionaries who may create new business products and services alongside the business unit leaders. In these cases, the CIO role may be perceived differently by superiors and peers within the enterprise and may be measured by thought leadership, rather than by technology solution delivery.

Whether a CIO fits one archetype or is a hybrid, renaissance leader, key expectations are cast by the organization and executive to whom the CIO reports. It is ideal, however, for the CIO to set expectations for himself/herself beyond those described by others for proactive career positioning.

Some key expectations for the CIO role include the following list of items offered in no order of preference:

- Provides policy, standards, and oversight for all IT concerns.
- Serves as a contributing team member of executive management.
- Develops strategic direction and integration of enabling IT to support organizational strategy.
- Aligns organization with an appropriate portfolio to its "IT identity."
- Offers proactive consultation and education to executive staff.

- Manages resources to delivery and expected outcomes.
- Recruits, retains, and mentors technology/management-competent professionals.
- Maintains organizational focus on data management principles, integration, and related workflows.
- Values customers.
- Leads in a manner consistent with organizational culture.

Examples of these 10 attributes in action are offered in the sections that follow.

Provides Policy, Standards, and Oversight for All IT Concerns

The CIO is responsible for IT policy leadership in most organizations. That responsibility and authority is a matter of organizational expectation, and yet the CIO is often positioned to author how the role affects such responsibility. For instance, the CIO will likely offer thoughts on how IT governance is put into place with management, be a key architect for chartering that body, and may chair or co-chair the IT governance group once defined. Policies and standards typically flow through this body for review and approval. Further, this body may establish organization expectations for IT business case development and review, have a strong voice in deciding those priorities that are budgeted, make decisions regarding board messaging, and even provide some degree of additional oversight to the many project-related steering groups that may exist.

The CIO is also responsible for putting IT planning activities in place, typically in concert with other enterprise planning and budgeting activities and timing. He/she must decide what forums will be created to garner input and facilitate the planning activities. Often, a key user-based committee is best for collecting candidate ideas and fostering business case development. Further, an infrastructure-focused team may be useful in describing the roadmaps necessary for well-planned design of the foundation elements upon which applications reside (i.e., networks, databases, computing assets, storage, data center, business recovery, security).

Finally, along with senior leadership, most CIOs will be expected to provide assurance reporting to the governance board. Some boards will prefer this function be done through a named committee to provide adequate focus on the IT agenda. This reporting venue is important to the CIO, as it is one whereby IT business unit capabilities, gaps, and delivery efforts and outcomes to assure the organization's mission through technology uses are highlighted.

Figure 1-1 provides a graphical depiction for an example IT governance structure.

Serves as a Contributing Team Member of Executive Management

The CIO position most often reports to the chief executive officer (CEO), chief operating officer (COO), or chief financial officer (CFO). A 2008 Forrester Research survey indicates that the percentage of CIOs reporting to the CFO has shrunk and that most now report to the CEO.[6] As important, the trust between CIO and his/her boss is vital for ongoing success.

More important than to whom the position reports is that the role be viewed as important to key team members and the board. The CIO is to be positioned with authority to act and the associated accountabilities and responsibilities that coincide.

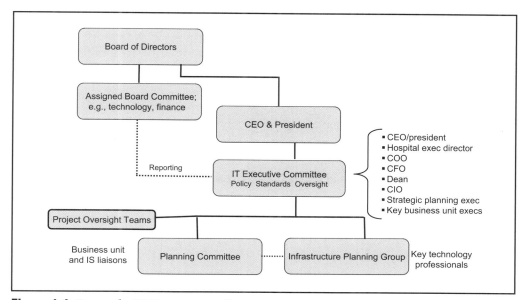

Figure 1-1: Example IT Governance Structure

Some CIOs have responsibility for the IT department. The IT team may comprise several hundred people working across many functional and technical elements of IT lifecycle concerns; "department" certainly seems an understatement of its relevance within the enterprise. IT growth being what it is, the IT business unit today may not only be larger in staff and budget size than 5 to 10 years ago, it may also include telecommunications, clinical engineering, health information management, informatics, materials management, or other functions a CIO's competencies may best exploit for delivering organizational business objectives.

The CIO should, hopefully, serve within key decision-making bodies of executive management, serve in IT and non-IT oversight roles, have appropriate board and board committee interactions, and offer leadership beyond those things technical. To be an effective member of the leadership team, the CIO must bring skills and competencies and also be positioned by culture, reporting relationship, audiences, and influence to add value.

Develops Strategic Direction and Integration of Enabling IT to Support Organizational Strategy

Setting the strategic direction for IT use is required of the CIO. This carries the implication that the IT uses will be consistent with the themes of organizational strategy. If they are not, the ideas should likely be discarded. Further, the requirement expects that the CIO will implement an IT planning process to deliver the enabling IT elements for the organization.

Figure 1-2 shows a number of elements in an IT plan for a care delivery organization (CDO).[7p48] This is one classic output of an IT plan. This example provides several insights into the decision process for crafting the IT strategic direction.

#	Area	Candidate Initiative	Entity	Project Sponsor	Executive Sponsor	Anticipated IT Plan Year	Organization Risk Assessment	Implementation Risk Assessment	Hype Cycle Phase	IT Guiding Principles
1	Academic	Student Information System	College	S. Snead	E. Wana	2008	2.5	2.7	A	✓
2	Business	Employee Satisfaction Survey System	Center	E. Ainge	R. Dobolino	2008	2.8	2.7	B	✓
3	Business	Workforce Central Timekeeper	Center	H. Hickman	R. Dobolino	2008	1.7	3.0	A	✓
4	Business	Security System Redeaux	Center	H. Hickman	R. Dobolino	2008	1.3	1.9	A	✓
5	Business	Bar Code Printers for Materials	Center	P. Matthews	R. Santoli	2007/2008	1.3	1.4	A	✓
6	Business	Digital Imaging - HR	Center	E. Ainge	R. Dobolino	2008	2.5	2.3	A	#4
7	Business	Materials Warehousing System	Center	P. Matthews	G. Hickman	2007/2008	1.3	1.4	A	✓
8	Business	Building Security	Center	D. Matthew	G. Hickman	2008	1.2	1.9	A	✓
9	Business	Critical Events Text Paging / Email Alert Module	Center	D. Matthew	G. Hickman	2008	1.3	1.9	A	✓
10	Business	Facility Maintenance Building/Equipment PM Management	Center	C. Harrison	R. Dobolino	2007/2008	1.5	1.7	A	✓
11	Business	Infant Abduction Protection System (Sunset replacement)	Center	E. Ainge	R. Santoli	2008	1.3	2.3	D	#5
12	Business	Electronic Bed Management and Census Control Board [3]	Finance	H. Sandwich	M. Bags	2008	2.2	3.6	NR	NR
18	Business	Enterprise Imaging - EHR [4]	Finance Hospital	C. Smith	M. Bags	2008	2.7	4.0	A	✓
19	Clinical	Enterprise EHR Hospital Initiative (Soarian)	Hospital	E. Gallo	D. Smith	2008	2.2	2.7	C	
20	Clinical	ED Management System (sunset)	Hospital	C. Monkee	N. Nursey	2008	2.0	3.4	B	✓
21	Clinical	Radiology Voice Recognition	Hospital	P. Carls	Y. Tittle	2008	1.7	1.6	A	✓
22	Clinical	Barcoded Specimen Collection	Hospital	M. Arthur	Y. Tittle	2008	2.0	2.3	B	# 6
23	Clinical	MSOW Replacement	Hospital	D. Matthew	M. Welby	2008	1.7	1.4	A	✓
24	Clinical	Employee Health EHR	Hospital	S. Claude	P. Manning	2008	2.2	2.7	A	#4
25	Business - Clinical	EHR PDA Support	Hospital	S. Claude	L. Filhour	2008	1.3	1.9	C	# 5
26	Clinical	Nuclear Medicine Pharmacy Information System	Hospital	A. Drugs	B. Pedlow	2008	1.2	1.6	NR	NR
28	Clinical	GI RN Documentation Module	Hospital	J. Love	N. Nursey	2008	2.0	2.3	A	✓
29	Clinical	PACU and Pre Op Expansion	Hospital	L. LaBlanc	N. Nursey	2008	1.7	1.6	B	✓
30	Clinical	Critical Care Module	Hospital	L. LaBlanc	N. Nursey	2009	NR	NR	C	# 5
31	Clinical	EHR Practice Initiative	Practice	J. DePen	B. Ditti	2008	2.2	2.7	B	✓
32	Clinical	Self Registration Kiosks	Practice Finance Hospital	K. Savage	B. Ditti	2008	1.7	2.6	C	#4

CDO Strategic Relevance columns (shown graphically as Harvey balls): Market Share Growth, Physician Alliances, Education & Research Mission, Quality Impact, Workforce Strategy, Philanthropy, Facilities / Space Planning, Information Technologies.

Source: The Healthcare IT Planning Fieldbook, Hickman and Smaltz, HIMSS, 2008.

Figure 1-2: **Example IT Annual Plan Portfolio**

First, each initiative is sponsored by a business unit leader. Good CIOs fully understand that the CIO, while a chief architect of the plan elements, must have the business unit energies required to design and deliver notable IT initiatives. Further, the business unit leaders are confronted with the economic imperatives for the enterprise, including the choices that must be made between IT, biomedical equipment, space needs, capital improvements, and new programs. Sponsorship is the cornerstone to placing an IT initiative on the organization's strategy map.

Second, a good planning process will require business case development for its candidate elements. The business case will usually cause the following to be articulated:

- Narrative description of the initiative, including current state practices and concerns and contrasting, desired state expectations.
- A time horizon that the effort is measured across, which may include multi-phasing for the effort.
- Projects and organizational risks associated with moving through the change.
- Quantitative and qualitative benefits, both one-time and ongoing.
- Total cost of ownership.
- Capability to support within the current state versus necessity to grow additional IT competencies and technologies.
- Abilities of workforce members to utilize the enabling technologies as per technology competency and workflow implications.
- Descriptions as to how the initiatives support key enterprise strategies.
- Portfolio "fit" or alignment as to agree with the organization's IT decision-making principles, including blend of early/leading edge versus current state technologies.
- Others as appropriate to the enterprise's needs.

Structuring the business case to a template approach assures like-comparison across candidate initiatives. Further, that will allow the introduction of scoring tools for elements, such as risk "fit" and strategic relevance, as shown in Figure 1-2.

Similarly, structuring the planning process itself is sound practice. Structure provides opportunity for all parties to understand how IT decisions will be made and, as appropriate, participate in the same. A structured planning cycle is also typically aligned with the annual budget cycle for the enterprise, creating certain efficiencies and assuring that all organizational priorities are co-examined. It is typical to predict a three-to-five-year plan and then refresh that plan during the annual cycle to newly understood realities. Figure 1-3 provides an example of a structured planning process.[7p5]

Aligns Organization with an Appropriate Portfolio to Its "IT Identity"

In tough economic times, establishing means to blend your personal investment portfolio is most challenging. A market analyst or financial planner should establish advice regarding your investment portfolio based upon your goals—such as expected growth, security or risk, immediate or long-range return, and other such factors.

The IT planning process or any organization's capital investment process is analogous to personal financial planning. The challenge or difference is that the organization has to define its goals and expectations for return. Defining IT expectations requires that the organization be able to articulate its "IT identity."

This may be somewhat measured but is mostly an intuitive notion. Figure 1-4 provides some example characteristics as may be used to define IT identity.[7p28] The organization may have hybrid behaviors relative to these characteristics, yet will need to understand where its behaviors are centered. Key decision makers regarding IT elements must be able to understand where its capabilities are centered and where variance is appropriate, acceptable, and manageable.

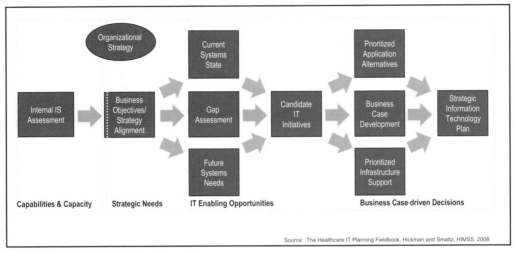

Source: The Healthcare IT Planning Fieldbook, Hickman and Smaltz, HIMSS, 2008.

Figure 1-3: IT Planning Lifecycle

IT Personality	Emerging, leading or bleeding edge	Measured benefits	Necessary evil
Approach to IT	Aggressive	Optimized and balanced	Cautious
Uses for IT	Strategic advantage	Consolidation and productivity garnering	Utility
Risk Tolerance	High	Moderate	Low
IT Metrics	Strategic advantage	Value-based	Efficiency
IT Investment Behaviors	"Executive jewelry" and "bet the farm"	"All things in moderation"	"Cost of doing business"

Source: The Healthcare IT Planning Fieldbook, Hickman and Smaltz, HIMSS, 2008.

Figure 1- 4: Example Characteristics for Defining IT Identity

The characteristics that comprise identity may also provide insight into how the organization approaches application or infrastructure needs. Ultra-conservative case delivery organizations (CDOs) with cost efficiency characteristics may have once opted for a "single vendor" approach to resolving its IT needs. This is increasingly difficult as IT needs are prolific. Thus, "best of family" and "best of class" approaches are more likely. However, it is fair to generalize that our industry is likely centered on "best of family" as an approach, except when the vendor family does not offer a solution. Each organization, however, must find its own place with this concept if it is to be used to construct a more aligned decision approach. Figure 1-5 shows the relationship of the single, best of family, and best of class approach to desired benefits. These relationships are useful to challenge investment and risk-bearing capacity.[7p40]

Desired Benefit	Single Vendor	Best of Family	Best of Class
Functional use best-fit	√	√√√	√√√
Ease of technology infrastructure supportability	√√√	√√	√
Vendor management and partnering	√√√	√√	√
Ease of integration efforts	√√√	√√	√
Inter-application workflow efficiencies	√√√	√√	√
Key: More √√√ indicates likelihood of best fit to the Desired Benefit			

Source: The Healthcare IT Planning Fieldbook, Hickman and Smaltz, HIMSS, 2008.

Figure 1-5: High-level Comparison of Selection Approaches

Another way to look at a portfolio's fit to an IT identity is to compare value to risk, again for the sake of assuring the decision makers agree that blend is appropriate. Figure 1-6 provides such an example comparison in scatter-gram form.[7p31] The quadrant-based figure shows the potential benefits and risk of several plotted technology initiatives.

IT guiding principles can be the basis for garnering decision-making alignment. Guiding principles can be expressed on the classic phases of an IT life cycle: Planning, Selection and Acquisition, Implementation, and On-going Support. A few examples of such principles are:

- **Planning:** "Our major IT decisions will expect a fully developed business case and total cost of ownership and will compete for resources with all other major organization investments."
- **Selection and Acquisition:** "We will bias our decision toward core and fewer vendors that can bring more fully integrated solutions versus best of breed vendors."
- **Planning:** "We will annually review and consider the amount of risk and return we are placing in our IT portfolio."

- **On-going Support:** "We will expect that IT-supported operational efforts will promulgate policies, processes, and performance metrics that support our enterprise business and clinical objectives."

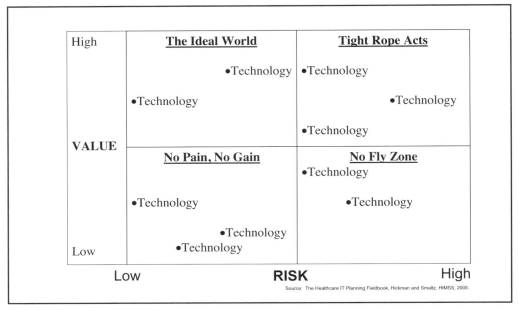

Figure 1-6: Example Candidate Portfolio Comparison for Benefit/Risk

Additionally, the portfolio can be represented in terms of current state and potential solutions. Figure 1-7 provides an example academic health system portfolio concept diagram, shaded to represent the state of implementation (or not) for the noted elements. This diagram is not exhaustive as to IT possibilities but provides a good generalized starting point.

Figure 1-8 provides a drill-down on one of the key mega-solution areas, revenue cycle-related systems. By articulating such key capabilities, the CIO can then identify those elements that currently exist from those planned or from those that should be highly considered for the opportunities they present. For this example, the CFO would be vital in aligning any agreement to sponsor a decision-making discussion for such elements.

Many outside analyst firms and other sources may also provide tools to assist in decision making, including HIMSS Analytics™, Forrester Research, Gartner, and HHN's Most Wired. Figure 1-9 shows an academic CDO's application portfolio benchmark as compared with the academic/teaching hospital sector.[7pp34-38] This HIMSS Analytics comparison can be drawn from the HIMSS/HIMSS Analytics Annual Report data. This benchmark can be developed for most of the solution portfolio available, as the Annual Report is quite exhaustive. The portfolio benchmark is useful in understanding how the CDO's portfolio compares with industry norm and will generate discussion of acceptance or need for change. The HIMSS Analytics EMR Adoption Model[SM] may also provide a useful comparison.

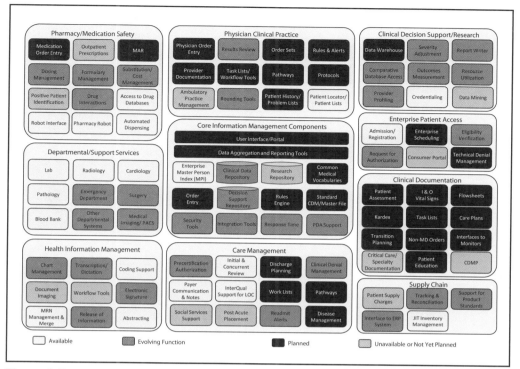

Figure 1-7: Example Portfolio for an Academic Health System

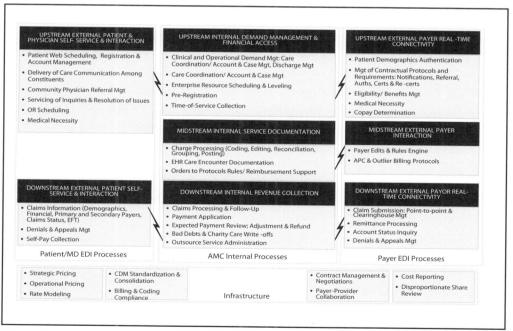

Figure 1-8 : Available Revenue Cycle Supporting Solutions

Applications by Area	2006 Academic / Teaching % Planned, Contracted, In Progress, In Use	CDO 2006 Status	2007 Academic / Teaching % Planned, Contracted, In Progress, In Use	CDO 2007 Status
Revenue Cycle				
Credit/Collections	88%	○	92%	◑
ADT/Registration	98%	●	99%	●
EDI-Clearinghouse	32%	●	43%	●
Electronic Claims	97%	●	NR	●
Eligibility	49%	○	62%	◑
Patient Billing	97%	●	99%	●
Contract Management	76%	◑○	76%	◑●
Enterprise Master Person Index	29%	◔	40%	●
Patient Scheduling	80%	◑○	89%	●○
Financial Decision Support Environment				
Budgeting	88%	●	89%	●
Case Mix Management	95%	●	93%	●
Cost Accounting	87%	◑	88%	●
Data Warehouse/Mining-Financial	26%	○	31%	○
Executive Information Systems	62%	○	61%	○

Not Available and Not Budgeted/Committed
Contracted/Planned
Implementing or Replacing
Implemented with Partial Adoption
Functional – Implemented

Source: 2007 HIMSS Analytics Annual Report of the U.S. Hospital IT Market; sample size ranges from 203-333 not-for-profit, academic/teaching hospitals in the U.S.

Figure 1-9: Application Portfolio Benchmark Using HIMSS Analytics Data

Offers Proactive Consultation and Education to Executive Staff

The CIO can be routinely viewed as the chief resident "geek." Many end-use questions are often asked in the hallways, not dissimilar to physician colleagues being asked all manner of medical consult questions at the neighborhood block party.

The CIO, however, may be well-positioned to provide proactive consultation on all forms of technology, data integration, process and workflow, and other such solution-related matters. Clearly, the CIO can be a leader in the C-suite in offering expert opinion as to technology trends, opportunities, risks, and the organizational needs.

However, the CIO may be a strategist in seeing opportunities that may exist beyond the bounds of technology concern. Routine executive dialogue may include:

- Change management implications in large-scale initiatives.
- Strategies for technology-change adoption.
- Functional process change explanations.
- Secure-design approaches to offer organizational assurance.
- Vendor market and solution performance.
- Key industry trends and IT implications.
- Governmental and regulatory changes and resulting organizational directions.
- Market factors that may influence technology alternatives and plans.
- Oversight advice regarding notable project activities.

Additional practical matters require the attention, and often the sponsorship, of the CIO. For example, the CIO may be the executive that nurtures such efforts as:

- Development of enterprise-wide IT competencies across the workforce.
- Development and support of a project management life cycle approach, including courseware, supporting tools, and performance evaluation expectations.

- "Show and tell" episodes for solutions for workforce members, management staff, or board-level audiences.
- Positioning discussions on solution-based topics that newly introduced technologies may bring, so that potential business and clinical sponsors have opportunity for greater understanding and the choice to lead.

Manages Resources to Delivery and Expected Outcomes

As any C-suite executive, the CIO is responsible and accountable for utilizing the CDO's resources to the best possible delivery and outcomes. Business case-based approaches to IT initiatives are certainly helpful toward this goal, as the expectations and measures for success are recorded and an eventual look-back can occur.

Program management of a portfolio supports this goal as well. Collective project expectations can be measured by how select areas meet intentions. These would include:

- Application delivery intentions as originally conceived.
- Functional and process changes.
- Timing.
- Contract management.
- Integration via data exchange and workflow.
- Technology expectations.
- Entity-scope.
- Infrastructural design/delivery.

Cost and value measurement are also CIO key outcome measures for most CDOs. Figure 1-10 provides a summary table as drawn from a complex portfolio managed benefits/TCO model for management and board approval.[8] Delivery to this sort of framework provides the basis for annual review across a long-term, collective program effort.

AMC Master Agreement Preliminary Cash Flow Includes 3% CPI	Fees	2005 Annual Total	2006 Annual Total	2007 Annual Total	2008 Annual Total	2009 Annual Total	2010 Annual Total	2011 Annual Total
TOTAL DIRECT CONTRACTED COSTS		3,321,324	4,707,138	4,395,527	4,681,494	7,158,277	6,358,955	5,802,338
TOTAL NON CONTRACTED COSTS		267,375	5,606,626	11,269,299	10,880,090	11,040,098	11,481,500	8,277,607
TOTAL CONTRACT AND MODEL COST								
Total Operating		2,631,365	3,013,403	3,608,267	5,693,124	9,997,333	11,212,650	11,923,409
Total Capital		957,334	7,300,361	12,056,558	9,868,460	8,201,042	6,627,804	2,156,536
Total CashFlow		3,588,699	10,313,764	15,664,826	15,561,584	18,198,375	17,840,455	14,079,945
Less Legacy		2,573,238	2,474,181	2,476,462	2,550,733	2,528,773	1,425,609	381,627
Total CashFlow Less Legacy		1,015,461	7,839,583	13,188,364	13,010,850	15,669,602	16,414,846	13,698,317

Source: HIMSS Webcast: Building the EHR Total Cost of Ownership (TCO) Model, June 2006, Hickman, Kusche.

Figure 1-10: Cost Model Development

Recruits, Retains, and Mentors Technology and Management Competent Professionals

Success rides upon a key asset—your people. A CIO recently shared that the highest compliment he was paid in recent times was by an executive recruiter who was supporting a search for one of his executive direct report positions. The recruiter ended internal interviews with the question, "What is it like to work for your boss?" He shared with the CIO that the individuals shared their pride in working for the CIO because of his leadership, the high standard that he sets, the direction that he has given the organization, his profile in the industry, and his care for people. The recruiter went on to say that while the comments regarding the CIO were exemplary, his own perceptions of the CIO's leadership team were that they clearly functioned as a team; well-articulated the attributes they desire in a new colleague; held themselves and their colleagues to high professional and performance standards; and were very loyal to the organization, its mission and the values espoused by the IT business unit. It is the latter comments that mattered the most to this particular CIO.

Many leadership and management books are written on the importance of people and team in creating high-performing organizations. Those thoughts are best left to those who are learned in the space of that literature. To the point offered in these brief thoughts regarding the role of the CIO, the following tenets are offered:

- You are your team.
- The key to successful leadership today is influence, not authority.—Ken Blanchard
- The first responsibility of a leader is to define reality. The last is to say "thank you."—Max Dupree

Maintains Organizational Focus on Data Management Principles, Integration and Related Workflows

Data management is a prerequisite for good information management and decision making. The concepts of data management, including the following, hold true for any organizational level of discussion:

- Data definition.
- Data sources or sources of truth.
- Data security.
- Data uses.
- Data integration.

Further, beyond integration are the workflow impacts resulting from good or poor data exchanges between disparate systems. Many lessons learned have resulted from the outcomes of such integration efforts.

Figure 1-11 provides an example data integration schematic for an ambulatory electronic health record (EHR) initiative.[9] The diagram illustrates the number of data exchanges that must be put into place to have a fully functional EHR to support the physician practice setting. The approach does not consider technologies, such as single sign-on (SSO) and context management (beyond proprietary tools as may be demonstrated). Certainly the diagram's "business" connotes the amount of data exchange that must occur to assure EHR primacy in physician workflow.

Values Customers

CIOs value their customer, who may be many and have varied and even competing needs. Some of the key IT processes supporting customer service are noted in Figure 1-12. In this case, they are placed on a measured scale representing four process capabilities: Firefighting, Reactive, Proactive, or Leading Practice.

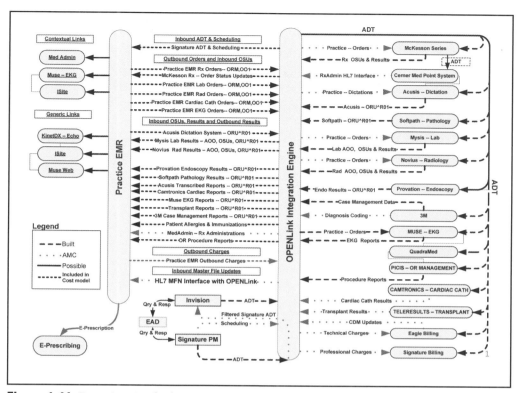

Figure 1-11: Practice Ambulatory EMR High-level Conceptual Integration Diagram

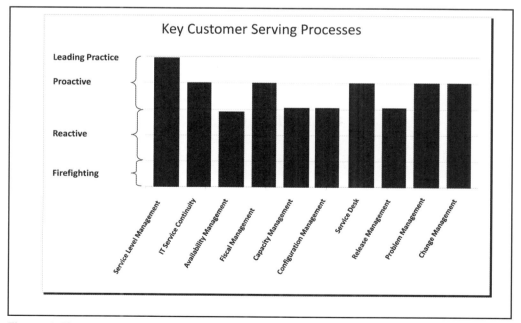

Figure 1-12: Key Customer Serving Processes

Establishment of agreed measures and target performance levels is important to customer service. Some IT business units will derive measures, put them into place, and publish performance routinely on an internal Web page. Others may establish service level objectives (SLOs) for key customer serving elements and seek to gain agreement as to performance levels with the customers. Others may yet develop service level agreements (SLAs) in which the measures become formalized, as well as the role-interplay that must occur between IT and customer constituents for successful delivery. The "best" way to approach a customer measurement effort will be a feature of organizational culture.

Customer service comes from leadership philosophy. It is also generated by workforce members who have values that naturally generate customer service behaviors. It is much easier to hire a team that has customer concern (and other values) than to seek to train these attributes.

Several tenets that may be useful to support customer service include:

- Speed to value; a sense of urgency is important.
- Be everywhere, do everything, and never fail to astonish the customer.—Macy's
- Focus on the journey, not the destination.—Greg Anderson
- The journey of a thousand miles often ends very badly.—Unknown
- Your most unhappy customers are your greatest source of learning.—Bill Gates

Leads in a Manner Consistent with Organizational Culture

Much of the CIO's energy is focused on creating organizational change. Hence, an understanding of enterprise culture is necessary to be an effective, executive change agent. CIO leadership should measure cultural implications to any change approach, and that knowledge should also be positioned for the benefit of assuring organizational and project/program success.

Culture can trump any strategy if not carefully considered into the plan. Culture is what translates the true values of an organization and its people, not the placard of values that are posted on the wall. Culture takes as long to change as it takes for people and patterns of behavior to transition through an organization. Hence, it is said that culture does not change, it only bends over time.

OTHER DIMENSIONS

There are many other dimensions and attributes that an organization may expect its ideal CIO to have. Table 1-3 offers some examples of such dimensions. While many of those attributes are common to any executive role, some may be more specific to a technology management leader. These are offered as additional insights as to how the hiring manager views personality and other characteristics for the CIO and others in the C-suite.

Table 1-3: Other CIO Dimensions and Attributes

• Keeps current with industry and technologies • Strong credible leader • Proactive/goal-oriented/ service-oriented • Excellent communication skills on all levels—board, management, physicians, staff • Demonstrated experience in managing differing user needs • Proven track record in providing service • Successful history of planning, implementing, and supporting systems in a complex, academic healthcare environment • High integrity • Team player and team leader • Approachable	• Sense of humor • Creative/innovative • Risk taker • Fiscally responsible and competent • Systems thinker • Excellent negotiating/ marketing skills at all levels • Proven experience at hiring and motivating talent • High energy level • Outstanding consensus builder • Keen read on organizational culture and mission • Forward thinking and seasoned professional • Capable at crafting and managing complex "vendor" deals

REFERENCES

1. *Guide to Effective Health Care Information and Management Systems and the Role of the Chief Information Officer.* ISBN 0-87258-497-6, HIMSS, 1987.

2. College of Healthcare Information Management Executives. The history of CHIME. http://www.cio-chime.org/chime/about/history.asp. Accessed November 12, 2009.

3. CIO is starting to stand for 'career is over.' *Business Week*, February 26, 1990, page 78.

4. CIOs are entering a career ice age. *Computer World*, January 12, 2009.

5. Koch C. Beyond execution. *CIO,* January 1, 2007.

6. Cameron, B. *CIOs: Reporting Relationship Defines Your Job Only at the Margins.* Forrester Research, July 16, 2008, http://www.forrester.com/Research/Document/Excerpt/0,7211,45697,00.html. Accessed November 12, 2009.

7. Hickman GT, Smaltz. *The Healthcare IT Planning Fieldbook.* HIMSS:Chicago, 2008, pps 5, 28, 31, 34-38, 40, 48.

8. Hickman GT, Kusche. *Building the EHR Total Cost of Ownership (TCO) Model.* HIMSS Webcast, June 2006.

9. Hickman GT. *Best Practices for EHR.* Presentation to World Healthcare Congress, April 2007.

CHAPTER 2

An Overview of the U.S. Health System and Public Policy Implications

By David W. Roberts, MPA, FHIMSS, and K. Meredith Taylor, MPH

INTRODUCTION: A GLIMPSE AT THE HEALTHCARE LANDSCAPE

Unfortunately, "efficient" and "effective" are not common descriptors of healthcare in the United States, which spends more on healthcare[1] and sustains a higher infant mortality rate[2] than any other industrialized country. U.S. healthcare is grossly inefficient, with higher healthcare spending not necessarily correlating with better outcomes and access to healthcare services.

In 2009, total healthcare spending in the United States was expected to reach $2.5 trillion, 17.6% of the gross domestic product (GDP),[3] up from $2 trillion in 2005.[4] By 2018, the Centers for Medicare & Medicaid Services (CMS) projects healthcare spending will be more than $4.3 trillion, accounting for 20.3% of the GDP.[5] The growing levels of healthcare spending correlate with the prevalence of chronic diseases, such as hypertension and diabetes and treatment of patients who are chronically ill. According to the Kaiser Family Foundation, about 45% of Americans suffer from one or more chronic diseases, accounting for 70% of deaths and approximately 75% of all healthcare spending.[5]

As healthcare spending increases, so does the rate of uninsured Americans, which currently stands at approximately 45 million,[3] an increase of 1 million from 2000.[6] The rising rate of uninsured Americans is the result of high unemployment levels,[7] the escalating cost of insurance premiums, lack of access to employer-sponsored healthcare coverage, and the inability to qualify for federal- and state-sponsored health coverage. This means that this population of uninsured Americans is more likely to skip recommended medical tests and treatments, forgo preventive healthcare services, and delay needed treatments.[6]

The aging baby-boomer population, combined with the increasing prevalence of Americans with disabilities and chronic diseases, place tremendous strains on publicly-funded healthcare programs, such as Medicare and Medicaid. Medicare, the entity which provides healthcare coverage to 45 million Americans who are 65 or older, disabled, or have end-stage renal disease, spends 14% of all federal dollars.[8] From 2006 to 2012, net federal spending on Medicare is projected to increase from $374 billion to $564 billion. The rising budget of the Medicare program is directly attributed to the composition of the program's beneficiaries and their rendered services:

- In 2005, 10% of beneficiaries accounted for more than two thirds of total Medicare spending.[8]
- Approximately one-third of beneficiaries have three or more chronic conditions.
- In-patient hospital stays comprise the program's largest portion of expenses.
- Approximately 2.2 million beneficiaries reside in long-term care settings.[9]

Serving as the nation's largest health coverage program, Medicaid covers an estimated 49.1 million low-income Americans, including families, people with disabilities, and elderly individuals. In 2007, Medicaid served approximately one in five Americans. In 2008, Medicaid spending reached nearly $339 billion, an increase of 7.3% over 2007. In the next 10 years, CMS expects expenditures to increase at an annual average rate of 7.9%, reaching $673.7 billion by 2017.[10] Nearly three quarters of Medicaid spending is attributed to one quarter of beneficiaries, primarily elderly and disabled individuals. The intense use of acute and long-term care services by these beneficiaries will continue to place an enormous strain on the program.[11,12]

In the United States, such high levels of healthcare spending do not always correlate with high-quality care. According to the Central Intelligence Agency's (CIA's) *2008 Fact Book*, the United States has the highest infant mortality rate (6.30) compared with other industrialized countries. Countries ranking higher (lower mortality rates) than the United States include Japan, United Kingdom, Hong Kong, Iceland, and France.[13] In addition, the U.S. Department of Health and Human Services' (HHS') Agency for Healthcare Research and Quality (AHRQ) estimates that the number of deaths from medical errors ranges from 44,000 to 98,000 a year.[14]

THE PROMISE OF HEALTH INFORMATION TECHNOLOGY

Health information technology (IT) shows promise for transforming the delivery of healthcare in the United States, improving population health and the overall efficiency and effectiveness of healthcare. *Health IT* can be defined as the use of computers and computer programs to store, protect, retrieve, and transfer clinical, administrative, and financial information electronically within and between healthcare stakeholders. Health IT is used in a variety of settings: in-patient (hospital, medical/surgical/long-term care, etc.); out-patient (ambulatory and specialty); life sciences; payers; public health; and others. Examples of health IT include:

- Electronic health records (EHRs)
- Electronic medical records (EMRs)
- Personal health records (PHRs)
- Payer-based health records (PBHRs)
- Electronic prescribing (e-Prescribing)
- Financial/billing/administrative systems
- Computerized practitioner order entry (CPOE) systems

The potential benefits of health IT are enormous. Appropriately implemented and utilized, health IT can enable better access to healthcare services and information, resulting in improved healthcare outcomes and cost savings. Medical errors can be reduced and time constraints nearly eliminated when a caregiver uses health IT to review medical records or order healthcare services. Health IT also enables consumers to better communicate with their providers and manage their personal health, resulting in fewer office visits and better disease management. Outside of a provider's office, health IT enables health information to be aggregated and applied to such activities as population health monitoring and disaster management, and optimizes payments for care.

The benefits of health IT can be broken down into two categories: "soft" return on investment (ROI) and "hard" ROI. Soft ROI addresses the benefits that are associated with patient safety, process improvement, and regulatory compliance. Hard ROI involves two measurements: quantifiable returns that can be demonstrated in financial terms and quality/process improvements that suggest cost savings that may fit an identifiable or measurable metric. Tables 2-1 and 2-2 detail examples of ROI experienced among hospitals and ambulatory care providers. The providers that are included in these tables are recipients of the HIMSS Nicholas E. Davies Award of Excellence.[15] Established in 1994, this program is a nationally-coveted award and peer-reviewed process founded upon the structure of the Malcolm Baldrige Award. Awards are granted on demonstrated excellence in implementation and proven derived ROI value from EHR/EMR systems, acting as model practices for others to emulate.

Table 2-1: Examples of Documented Soft Return on Investment from Use of EMR/EHR Systems[15]

Category	Examples
Patient Safety	• Maimonides Medical Center, a 705-bed hospital in New York City, saw problem medication orders drop by 58% and medication discrepancies by 55%. • Through use of an EMR/EHR system, 324-bed Cincinnati Children's Hospital decreased medication errors by 50% and achieved nearly zero mislabeled lab specimens. • At Ohio State University Health Systems, online medication charting errors in transcription dropped to zero for departments using an EMR/EHR system, versus transcription errors of 26% in departments not using the system.
Process Improvement	• Each physician at University of Illinois Chicago Medical Center saved five hours per week in time spent reviewing resident orders. • Cincinnati Children's decreased the time spent on the medication cycle entering orders, receiving orders, and shortening the care process for patients and staff by 52%. • In Chicago, Riverpoint Pediatrics decreased wait time by 36 minutes in all encounters—a 40% decrease. • Cooper Pediatrics of Duluth, Georgia decreased drug-refill wait times by 42% and lowered turnaround telephone call time by 75% (to less than 20 minutes).
Communications	• Queens Health Network applies the system for sharing documentation by all staff across the continuum of care, aiding in the elimination of duplication of activities. • Citizens Memorial in Bolivar, Missouri, eliminated the need for transport of documents by making the EMR/EHR system available from any of its care locations and hospital departments. "Message to Nursing" enables physicians to send patient instructions or information to a nurse.
Regulatory Compliance	• Ohio State University Health System advanced full compliance with institutional policies and bylaws regarding do-not-resuscitate orders and restraint orders. • Cincinnati Children's saw orders permanently unsigned by physicians drop from 40% to around 10% and witnessed a corresponding 24% drop in verbal orders.[16,17]

All examples above are from the Nicholas E. Davies Award. Established in 1994, the Davies Award – based upon the Baldrige National Quality Program – recognizes excellence in the implementation and value from health IT. There are four Davies Awards – Public Health, Organizational, Ambulatory, and Community Health Organizations. Additional information is available at http://www.himss.org/davies/index.asp.

Table 2-2: Examples of Documented Hard Return on Investment from Use of EMR/
EHR Systems[15]

Category	Example
Patient Flow	• Citizens Memorial of Bolivar, Missouri, saw net patient revenues increase 23%. • Brooklyn's Maimonides Medical Center experienced an increase in emergency department visits – from 57,795 in 1996 to 77,118 in 2002. In addition, length-of-stay declined from 7.26 days in 1995 to 5.05 days in 2001.
Materials and Staff Reductions	• Evanston Northwestern in Evanston, Illinois increased volume equivalent to eliminating 65 full-time employees throughout the corporation, or $4 million in savings. In addition, the hospital reduced personnel in the emergency department, medical records, and billing, and decreased overtime and temporary expenses, resulting in a total savings of $7.78 million. • In Decatur, Illinois, Heritage Behavioral Health saved $473,859 over three years in the following areas: $211,000 for transcription and documentation; $146,000 for chart audit paybacks; and $117,000 for back-office staffing reductions.
Billing Improvements	• Maimonides saw profits rise from $761,000 in 1996 to $6.1 million in 2001 as a result of improved bill collection. • Chicago's Riverpoint Pediatrics increased collection rates from 52% to 88% and eliminated claims denied due to coding errors. Insurance payment turnaround time fell from between 30 and 60 days, to approximately 15 days. • Southwest Texas Medical, in Beaumont, saw charges rise from $171 to $206 per patient encounter, a 20% jump. A year after implementation, the clinic's total billable hours increased by $2.1 million, while collections rose $1.4 million. • Citizens Memorial experienced a decrease in accounts receivable for its physicians from more than 80 days to fewer than 50 days by centralizing billing and charging functions, and consolidating the databases of 16 clinics.[16,17]
All examples above are from the Nicholas E. Davies Award. Established in 1994, the Davies Award – based upon the Baldrige National Quality Program – recognizes excellence in the implementation and value from health IT. There are four Davies Awards – Public Health, Organizational, Ambulatory, and Community Health Organizations. Additional information is available at http://www.himss.org/davies/index.asp.	

FOSTERING SMART BUSINESS PRACTICES IN HEALTHCARE

As policymakers strive to automate healthcare through such health information systems as EHRs, it is important that health information management systems are equally applied in healthcare to improve the performance of everyday administrative functions among payers and providers, such as processing claims and bills. According to McKinsey & Company,[18] the United States' healthcare system consumes more than 15% of total expenditures on processing payments. In addition, it is estimated that providers spend $100 billion or more a year in managing claims and $150 billion is spent among public and private payers.

While much of the high costs are associated with activities such as contract management and revenue cycle processes, one of the most important factors is the high cost of transmitting paper-based claims and payment of claims among payers and providers. McKinsey & Company[18] finds that approximately 60% of all claims payments are paper-based, involving paper claims that are sent between payers and providers manually submitting and reconciling claims and depositing checks. Paper-based claims cost approximately $8 per claim to process.

Each year in the United States, the volume of claim payments is 2.5 million. As the majority of reimbursements are based on paper checks, this costs healthcare $15 to $20 billion a year in postage, processing, and accounting. It is estimated that increasing the rate of electronic payment of claims to 90% from the current 40% could save $6 billion or more across the country.[18] Healthcare and the U.S. economy can no longer afford to wait to bring their business practices into the 21st century.

Policy Suggestion #1: Congress should mandate an end to the use of paper checks for reimbursement among payers and providers of federally-funded healthcare programs.

ASSISTING PROVIDERS IN THE ADOPTION AND USE OF HEALTH IT

While health IT holds great promise for healthcare in the United States, not all providers have the financial means to adopt and use health IT products. Unless the federal government continues to assist providers with the financial incentives to adopt and use health IT, healthcare is decades away from reaping the benefits of the widespread exchange of health information. In a recent survey conducted by HIMSS and HIMSS Analytics, approximately 30% of the 500 surveyed ambulatory care providers use some component of an EMR in their organization.[19] In addition, the HIMSS Analytics EMR Adoption Model[SM], based upon a census survey of 100% of medical/surgical non-federal hospitals in the United States, indicates that more than 80% of U.S. hospitals use some level of an EMR (see Figure 2-1).

EMR Adoption Model[SM]

Stage	Cumulative Capabilities	% of US Hospitals 2008 Q2	% of US Hospitals 2008 Q3
Stage 7	Medical record fully electronic; HCO able to contribute CCD as byproduct of EMR; Data warehousing in use	0.0%	0.1%
Stage 6	Physician documentation (structured templates), full CDSS (variance & compliance), full R-PACS	0.9%	1.0%
Stage 5	Closed loop medication administration	1.0%	1.3%
Stage 4	CPOE, CDSS (clinical protocols)	1.8%	1.9%
Stage 3	Clinical documentation (flow sheets), CDSS (error checking), PACS available outside Radiology	32.0%	32.9%
Stage 2	Clinical Data Repository, Controlled Medical Vocabulary, Clinical Decision Support System, may have Document Imaging	33.9%	33.2%
Stage 1	Ancillaries – Lab, Rad, Pharmacy - All Installed	12.6%	12.5%
Stage 0	All Three Ancillaries Not Installed	17.7%	17.1%

© 2008 HIMSS Analytics™

Figure 2-1: HIMSS Analytics EMR Adoption Model[SM]

The HIMSS Analytics EMR Adoption Model[SM] identifies the levels of EMR capabilities, ranging from the initial clinical data repository (CDR) environment through a paperless EMR environment. HIMSS Analytics can determine the level of EMR capabilities through a methodology and algorithms to score the 5,071 hospitals in its database relative to their progress in implementing the components of an EMR and to provide peer comparisons for care delivery organizations.

Recently with passage of the American Recovery and Reinvestment Act of 2009 (ARRA), Congress and President Obama took the first big steps in changing the way healthcare is delivered through the application of incentives. Through Medicare and Medicaid, ARRA requires that CMS reward providers for demonstrating a "meaningful use of certified EHR technology." The Congressional Budget Office (CBO) (http://www. cbo.gov/ftpdocs/99xx/doc9989/hr1conference.pdf) estimates the total cost of Medicare and Medicaid incentives for eligible professionals and hospitals that demonstrate a meaningful use of certified EHR technology to be $20.819 billion. This incentive total is derived from the sum of the total costs of the incentives in fiscal year 2009 to fiscal year 2015 ($36.368 billion) and the total savings that are achieved in fiscal year 2016 to fiscal year 2019 through the incentives ($15.549 billion). Through the new incentives programs, CBO estimates that approximately 70% of hospitals and 90% of physicians will have adopted qualifying health IT in 2019.[20] For eligible hospitals, the incentives will be available after October 1, 2010. For eligible professionals, incentives will be available after January 1, 2011.

In addition to new incentives programs established through ARRA, the act also made additional funding available to assist providers in adopting health IT. Specifically, ARRA established a new loan program, to be administered by states, to make available seed funding for providers to assist in the adoption of health IT. The program is directed to start sometime after January 2010.

According to some organizations, the potential savings from the widespread use of health IT could reach over $75 billion each year. For example, the RAND Corporation estimated that, if the U.S. healthcare system implemented the use of computerized medical records, the system could save more than $81 billion each year.[21] In addition, the Center for Information Technology Leadership (CITL) estimated that the implementation of national standards for interoperability and the exchange of health information would save the U.S. approximately $77 billion in expenses related to healthcare each year.[22]

Unfortunately, financial constraints inhibit many ambulatory and acute care providers (i.e., hospitals) from adopting health IT. According to some studies, the initial costs associated with adopting health IT are approximately $33,000[23] or $10,000 over a 3-year period.[24] In addition, HIMSS Analytics estimates that the average cost for civilian U.S. hospitals is approximately $13,529,000 to $19,585,000 billion to achieve Stage 4 of the HIMSS Analytics EMR Adoption Model.[SM]

In addition to funding available through CMS, additional federal agencies are working to foster the use of health IT among providers. For example, the Health Resources Services Administration (HRSA) and AHRQ are working to foster the use of health IT through the use of financial incentives, such as grants, loans, and increased reimbursement. Many of these programs are focused on those providers that serve the lowest-income Americans.

Policy Suggestion #2: To ensure that federal funds are used to their fullest extent, the federal government must authorize and appropriate funding for health IT in a strategic manner that will foster the wide-scale use of interoperable health IT and support the needs of underserved patient populations.

Another challenge among providers in effectively utilizing health IT relates to the financial aspects of supporting telehealth services. While telehealth should not be interpreted as a form of health IT, health IT is an enabling component of telehealth services. According to the American Telemedicine Association (ATA), *telehealth* refers to a method of care delivery and healthcare services over distances.[25]

Financial challenges surrounding telehealth services relate to infrastructure and reimbursement. Today, lack of funding inhibits many communities from having the proper telecommunications infrastructure, primarily access to broadband, to provide telehealth services that rely on tools such as EMRs, medical imaging, and video conferencing. In 2007, to aid public and non-profit healthcare providers in building state and regional broadband networks for telehealth, the Federal Communications Commission's (FCC's) Rural Health Care Pilot Program (RHCPP) dedicated more than $417 million to healthcare entities in 42 states and 3 U.S. territories.[26]

Policy Suggestion #3: Continued support and expansion of this program is essential for the long-term sustainability and growth of telehealth in the United States.

In addition to infrastructure, reimbursement for telehealth services is inadequate, inhibiting many providers from engaging in telehealth programs. Medicare is the key program providing reimbursement for telehealth services. Reimbursement for select telehealth services is also available among certain private health plans and some state Medicaid programs.[27] There are several demonstration programs that are in use today. Unless a state mandates for telehealth services to be covered by private health plans, reimbursement for telehealth services is available only through select Medicaid programs. Under Medicare, reimbursement for telehealth services is inconsistent among providers, services, and geographic regions. For example, even though telehealth can benefit any underserved community that lacks access to a specialized healthcare service, a foundational requirement for telehealth services under Medicare is that the service must be provided for outside of a metropolitan area. In addition, while telehealth holds great promise for home healthcare, Medicare does not reimburse for telehealth services delivered by home health agencies.

Policy Suggestion #4: It is essential that providers are recognized and reimbursed appropriately for their services that are delivered through telehealth.

EMPOWERING CONSUMERS THROUGH HEALTH IT

While there are many programs underway among federally-funded health programs that make health IT, such as PHRs and PBHRs, available to beneficiaries, there are no plans to ensure that all beneficiaries have access to such tools to better manage their health. Widespread use of health IT among beneficiaries would enable both the private and public sectors to empower consumers with health information through IT. Examples of such programs that are currently underway are through the Veterans Health Administration (VHA) and CMS.

Through the VHA, veterans can access their PHR, My Healthe-Vet, to enter information about their medical and personal histories, as well as keep personal logs concerning their cholesterol and blood sugar levels. Through these features, clinicians are able to maintain a more comprehensive health record on a patient. My Healthe-Vet also provides patients access to literature and other clinical information. In addition, patients can request prescription refills and even control who can see their information on the PHR.[28]

CMS is exploring the benefits of consumer-centric health IT. Through multiple pilot projects within Medicare, CMS is assessing the use of PHRs by identifying features that beneficiaries prefer and how a PHR can incorporate claims information from services outside of the program.[29,30] Also through CMS, many state Medicaid programs are using health IT to foster consumer engagement with their healthcare. For example, through a Medicaid Transformation Grant, Oregon Medicaid is working to improve the efficiency in healthcare delivery by providing beneficiaries with their own PHR that is facilitated through the Health Record Bank of Oregon (HRBO).[31]

Policy Suggestion #5: As Medicare and Medicaid continue to serve some of the most chronically ill patient populations, it is essential that the programs strategically empower the beneficiaries with health IT.

THE CLIMATE FOR HEALTHCARE REFORM

As depicted previously, healthcare in the United States will continue to operate at inefficient and unsustainable levels unless real reforms are implemented to transform the delivery of care. The 111th Congress is actively addressing healthcare reform through the introduction and consideration of comprehensive healthcare reform legislation and the facilitation of hearings to address the issue.

As part of his campaign, President Barack Obama's healthcare proposal included many measures aimed at improving the overall quality, efficiency, and access to healthcare. Aspects of then-candidate Obama's campaign proposal included:

- Provide for affordable and high-quality universal coverage through a mix of private and expanded public insurance.
- Require that all children have health insurance.
- Require insurance companies to cover pre-existing conditions.
- Create tax credits to help small businesses provide affordable health insurance to their employees.
- Establish a National Health Insurance Exchange to help individuals and small businesses buy affordable health coverage.
- Invest $50 billion toward the adoption of EMRs and other health IT.
- Improve the prevention and management of chronic conditions.
- Reform medical malpractice.
- Expand the primary care provider and public health practitioner workforce.
- Reduce healthcare costs by allowing the importation of safe medicine.[32]
- Expand funding to ensure a strong workforce that will champion prevention and public health activities.[33]

As president, Barack Obama included health IT as part of an economic stimulus package passed by Congress, which he signed into law (P.L. 111-5, ARRA) on February 17, 2009.[34] President Obama repeatedly referred to the investment in health IT, made possible through ARRA, as a foundation for healthcare reform.

In the 111th Congress, members of Congress are actively engaged in healthcare reform deliberations. For example, in November 2008, Senator Max Baucus (D-MT) released a report entitled "Call to Action," which detailed priorities and next steps for healthcare reform. Also in November, then Senator Edward Kennedy (D-MA) announced the formation of three work groups within the U.S. Senate Health, Education, Labor, and Pensions Committee to deal with critical issues of healthcare reform, such as prevention and public health, quality, and insurance coverage.

In addition, in 2009, the committees of jurisdiction on healthcare reform matters (House Energy and Commerce, Ways and Means, and Education and Labor, and the Senate Finance and Health, Education, Labor, and Pensions [HELP] Committees) each considered healthcare reform legislation and held hearings on the issue. In the House, leading healthcare reform legislation is entitled the "Affordable Health Choices Act," which among many things, proposes a public option to expand healthcare coverage to Americans and a host of provisions that aim to leverage health IT in expanding access to care and improving the overall quality of care. In the Senate, two pieces of the legislation were developed—one by the Senate Finance Committee and another by the Senate HELP Committee, with the end goal of developing a comprehensive piece of legislation for consideration by the Senate. The Affordable Health Choices Act, developed by the Senate HELP Committee, also includes a public option and a handful of health IT provisions.

The America's Healthy Future Act proposes an alternative to a public option: the development of regional cooperatives to facilitate a low-cost health insurance option, as well as provisions that aim to leverage health IT in improving the overall efficiency of healthcare. Common issues addressed in legislation, as it pertains to health IT, include the application of health IT in capturing quality measurements, the application of incentives to reward providers for using health IT, and an increase in health IT training within the healthcare workforce.

Leaders in Congress are working to complete healthcare reform legislation in 2010. No matter the outcome this year, efforts to reform healthcare are sure to remain a top priority.

Policy Suggestion #6: The Obama administration and Congress must continue to work toward transforming the delivery and access to healthcare in the United States through the application of health IT.

CONCLUSION

As policymakers engage in deliberations concerning healthcare reform with the goal of re-creating a functional U.S. healthcare system, *it is essential that health IT is integrated into any healthcare reform proposal*. Health IT is a pivotal tool in transforming the delivery and payment of healthcare, holding opportunities to improve the access and quality of healthcare, while decreasing the costs, empowering consumers in their healthcare decisions, and enhancing the privacy and security of personal health information.

When incorporating health IT in healthcare reform policy, it is important that policymakers address some of the top priority issues facing the widespread integration of health IT in healthcare, such as leadership, interoperability, privacy and security, and funding. Policymakers should consider suggestions concerning each of these priority issues to strengthen and sustain the success of their healthcare reform legislation, proposals, and regulation policies.

REFERENCES

1. *Health Care Costs 101-2005.* California Health Care Foundation. March 2, 2005. http://www.chcf.org/. Accessed November 12, 2009.

2. Rank Order- Infant Mortality Rate. *2008 CIA Fact Book.* https://www.cia.gov/library/publications/the-world-factbook/rankorder/2091rank.html. Accessed November 5, 2009.

3. *Healthcare Costs and the Election, 2008.* The Kaiser Family Foundation. Health08.org. http://www.kff.org/insurance/h08_7828.cfm. Accessed November 4, 2009.

4. *Healthcare Costs, A Primer: Key Information on Healthcare Costs and their Impact.* Kaiser Family Foundation. August 2007. http://www.kff.org/insurance/upload/7670.pdf. Accessed November 5, 2009.

5. *Trends in Healthcare Costs and Spending.* Kaiser Family Foundation. March 2009. http://www.kff.org/insurance/upload/7692_02.pdf. Accessed December 12, 2009.

6. *The Uninsured and Their Access to Healthcare.* Medicaid and the Uninsured. The Henry J. Kaiser Family Foundations. http://www.kff.org/uninsured/loader.cfm?url=/commonspot/security/getfile.cfm&PageID=13335. Accessed November 20, 2009.

7. Impact on Unemployment Growth on Medicaid and SCHIP and the Number of Uninsured. *Kaiser Fast Facts.* The Henry J. Kaiser Family Foundation. http://slides.kff.org/chart.aspx?ch=360. Accessed November 3, 2009.

8. *Medicare Spending and Financing.* Medicare. The Henry J. Kaiser Family Foundation. http://www.kff.org/medicare/upload/7305_03.pdf. Accessed November 20, 2009.

9. *Medicare, A Primer.* March 2007. The Henry J. Kaiser Family Foundation. http://www.kff.org/medicare/upload/7615.pdf. Accessed November 5, 2009.

10. *2008 Actuarial Report on the Outlook for Medicaid.* Centers for Medicare and Medicaid Services, U.S. Department of Health and Human Services. http://www.cms.hhs.gov/ActuarialStudies/downloads/MedicaidReport2008.pdf. Accessed November 20, 2009.

11. *Medicaid Spending Growth and Options for Controlling Cost.* Congressional Testimony, Congressional Budget Office, Acting Director, Donald B. Marron. http://www.cbo.gov/ftpdocs/73xx/doc7387/07-13-Medicaid.pdf. Accessed November 5, 2009.

12. *The Medicaid Program at a Glance.* Kaiser Commission on Medicaid and the Uninsured. The Henry J. Kaiser Family Foundation. http://www.kff.org/medicaid/upload/7235-02.pdf . Accessed November 1, 2009.

13. Rank Order- Infant Mortality Rate. *2008 CIA Fact Book.* https://www.cia.gov/library/publications/the-world-factbook/rankorder/2091rank.html. Accessed November 1, 2009.

14. *Medical Errors, the Scope of the Problem.* U.S. Department of Health and Human Services, Agency for Healthcare Research and Quality. http://www.ahrq.gov/qual/errback.htm. Accessed November 1, 2009.

15. HIMSS Nicholas E. Davies Award of Excellence. http://www.himss.org/davies/index.asp. Accessed December 29, 2009.

16. *The ROI of EMR-EHR Productivity Soars, Hospitals Save Time and, Yes, Money.* HIMSS Nicholas E. Davies Award of Excellence. http://www.himss.org/content/files/davies/Davies_WP_ROI.pdf. Accessed November 1, 2009.

17. *Moving Ahead: EMR-EHR Drives Ambulatory Care.* HIMSS Nicholas E. Davies Award of Excellence. http://www.himss.org/content/files/davies/Davies_WP_Ambulatory.pdf. Accessed November 20, 2009.

18. *Overhauling the US Health Care Payment System.* McKinsey & Company. https://www.tipaaa.com/pdf/Overhauling%20the%20US%20Health%20Care%20Payment%20System-McKinsey%20Report.pdf. Accessed November 20, 2009.

19. *Ambulatory Healthcare IT Survey*. HIMSS Analytics. www.himssanalytics.org/docs/2008ambulatory_final.pdf. Accessed November 20, 2009.

20. Letter from Robert A. Sunshine, Acting Director of the CBO to the Honorable Charles Rangel, Chairman of the House Ways and Means Committee. http://www.cbo.gov/ftpdocs/99xx/doc9966/HITECHRangelLtr.pdf. Accessed December 29, 2009.

21. Hillestad, Richard and Bigelow, James H. Rand. *Health Information Technology: Can HIT Lower Costs and Improve Quality?* Rand Corporation. http://www.rand.org/pubs/research_briefs/RB9136/. Accessed November 1, 2009.

22. *The Value of Healthcare Information Exchange and Interoperability*. Center for Information Technology Leadership. Healthcare Information and Management Systems Society: Chicago, 2004.

23. Gans D, Kralewski J, Hammons T, Dowd B. *Medical Groups' Adoption of Electronic Health Records and Information Systems.* http://content.healthaffairs.org/cgi/content/full/24/5/1323. Accessed November 1, 2009.

24. Partners for Patients Electronic Health Record Market Survey. American Academy of Family Physicians Center for Health Information Technology. http://www.centerforhit.org/PreBuilt/chit_2005p4pvendsurv.pdf. Accessed November 20, 2009.

25. *Telemedicine, Telehealth, and Health Information Technology*. American Telemedicine Association. http://www.americantelemed.org/files/public/policy/HIT_Paper.pdf. Accessed November 5, 2009.

26. Rural Health Care Pilot Program. Universal Service Administrative Company. http://www.U.S.ac.org/rhc-pilot-program/tools/latest-news.aspx#111907. Accessed November 20, 2009.

27. *Private Payer Reimbursement for Telemedicine Services in the United States*. Department of Telecommunication. Michigan State University. http://www.americantelemed.org/files/public/policy/Private_Payer_Report.pdf. Accessed November 5, 2009.

28. Veteran's Health Administration: *The Best Value in Healthcare*. HIMSS Foundation. http://www.himss.org/foundation/docs/RachelMayo.pdf. Accessed November 20, 2009.

29. Health Plans Participate in CMS PHR Pilot to Help Medicare Beneficiaries Better Manage Their Health. America's Health Insurance Plans. http://www.ahip.org/content/pressrelease.aspx?docid=20043. Accessed November 3, 2009.

30. CMS Expands Personal Health Record Pilot in South Carolina to Include Data from TRICARE. Centers for Medicare and Medicaid Services. http://www.cms.hhs.gov/apps/media/press/release.asp?Counter=3275&intNumPerPage=10&checkDate=&checkKey=&srchType=1&nu. Accessed November 1, 2009.

31. *Overview of Medicaid Transformation Grant Centers for Medicare and Medicaid Services*. Oregon Health Record Bank. http://www.oregon.gov/DHS/hrb-oregon/project-info/overview1008.pdf. Accessed November 1, 2009.

32. *2008 Presidential Healthcare Proposals: Side-by-Side Summary*. Health08.org. The Henry J. Kaiser Family Foundation. http://www.health08.org/sidebyside_results.cfm?c=5&c=16. Accessed November 1, 2009.

33. Barack Obama and Joe Biden's Plan to Lower Health Care Costs and Ensure Affordable, Accessible Health Coverage for All. Obama for President. http://www.barackobama.com/pdf/issues/HealthCareFullPlan.pdf. Accessed November 20, 2009.

34. Obama Adds Health IT to Economic Stimulus Package. *Government Health IT*. http://www.govhealthit.com. Accessed November 1, 2009.

CHAPTER 3

Challenges Facing Hospitals: Perspectives of the CFO

By Raymond A. Gensinger, Jr., MD, CPHIMS, FHIMSS,
and Larry Kryzaniak, FHFMA

INTRODUCTION: NO MARGIN, NO MISSION

The chief financial officer (CFO) of an organization often has the most responsibility of the organizational leaders. The CFO has the responsibility of planning the healthcare organization's finances in an environment that is often equivalent to the shifting sands of a desert. The industry itself is one that, while relatively stable, can be affected by tremendous outside influence that is very difficult to predict and, when necessary, can be very difficult to adjust to. Balancing those shifting sands makes the difference between profit and loss and, therefore, whether there are available funds to continue the necessary investments of the organization to support its mission—thus, the expression which is often quoted: "no margin, no mission."

ROLE OF THE CFO: GLOBAL

The CFO of a healthcare organization maintains a great deal of responsibility trying to balance the funds of a very large organization in an ever-changing environment. Over the decades, the involvement of the CFO has had to evolve along with the support systems for reimbursement for large healthcare organizations. Going back 50 years, the systems of financial reimbursement were fairly limited; there were a limited number of insurance companies and secondary payers outside of the patients themselves.

The advent of Medicare, Medicaid, and ever more influential and powerful insurance companies compelled the need for greater and greater understanding of the complexity of healthcare financing, as the CFO and the organization became more invested in detailed cost accounting and more effective financial decision support systems for understanding the costs associated with patients and their diseases.

Many of the first enterprise-wide computing systems in healthcare were within the realm of the CFO. Originally, many of the hospitals' IT departments grew out of the management of the financial arm of the hospital or healthcare systems. Computers, mostly mainframes, were programmed with general ledger, billing and collections, insurance plan management, and any other functions that were designed to manage both the understanding of and the actual flow of money through the organization. Healthcare applications were limited, and many organizations began to build their own IT shops with responsibility for programming their own customized systems.

Over time, it was evident that the complexity of the financial market surrounding healthcare was increasing faster than many organizations could keep up with, and several software vendors began to move into the healthcare financial support market. Many healthcare systems migrated to these commercial applications, while others continued to manage their own software development shops. The CFO had to add to their skills the job of managing large IT company contracts, technology consultants, and a staff directly skilled in computers and computer programming. As those skills were developing, the vendors were evolving further. The largest and most successful of the financial systems vendors were beginning to dabble in the market of clinical systems as well. Those systems were in support of laboratories, radiology departments, biomedical electronic services, and other evolving high tech care areas of the hospital. Additionally, management of the organizational supply chain and the related explosion of costs associated with variation were also landing within the prevue of the CFO.

Now was the time for CFOs to again change their relationship with IT services in the hospital. The evolution of the chief information officer (CIO) was apparent, and the transition of management services for all technologies—financial and clinical, was moving to these CIOs. In some cases, the CFO would retain oversight for financial and supply-related systems, and the CIO began to have greater ownership of the clinical technologies, infrastructure, and biomedical electronics. The CFO's new role was to attend to the management of the integration of the organization's business plan, financial plan, and technology plan. Many CIOs were reporting to the CFO, and the coordination of these plans was an apparent necessity for the organization.

Clinical systems were growing and exceeding the necessity of financial systems to support a healthcare system's growth, quality, and financial strategies. Planning for the inclusion of these many new systems was complex, as an easy valuation formula was not always apparent. Calculating a true cost of ownership was vague in a formula based on dollars as the classic and only metric. Additionally, these systems came with extremely large price tags for the hardware, software, and professional services needed to get them effectively implemented and operational. These costs easily taxed an organization's capital planning and net cash flows because of the large depreciation expenses associated with the products themselves.

The CFO plays an important role in organizational governance trying to match the appetite for ever more complex and specific clinical systems within the financial capacity of the healthcare system. Departmental stakeholders can be very vocal and persuasive in their arguments for their system needs. It falls into the responsibility of the CFO to manage that appetite with all of the remaining financial needs of the organization and fairly balance all requests against the organizational goals. This often leads to controversy and requires an adept leader to communicate and enroll the organization toward common goals and objectives.

INFORMATION TECHNOLOGY VALUE MANAGEMENT

Valuing clinical IT and the associated necessary infrastructure (network, client PCs, and data centers) has been a challenge to many healthcare organizations because they offer little to no revenue to the organizations, are used inconsistently across the organizations, and often necessitate a sizeable staff to maintain. This is truly the construction of an internal utility company within the healthcare system.

The responsive CFO must understand the costs associated with the actual process of procuring, owning, and operating multiple organizational information systems for the organization over time. This is balanced against the knowledge, efficiencies, and quality improvements that can be generated by the same investments. The challenge, as stated earlier, is in trying to create a formula for determining the value of said system to the overall organization. In many ways, this process becomes almost as much a case of faith as it is one of fact. Formulas can be created to evaluate points at which associated efficiencies create opportunities to improve throughput or reduce the personnel resources necessary to complete tasks. Additionally, new data generated by these systems can feed into both financial and clinical decision support systems to gain a better understanding of the products used in delivering services and measure the varying costs of admissions in relation to the products that are being consumed within each of those admissions. Variance in process can be analyzed and standardized, where appropriated, to again have an effect on reducing organizational costs. Measuring quality can be achieved by changes in the number of errors that are recorded or in the outcomes of patients admitted with certain disease processes. The challenge comes in applying a value to that change in quality. In a world of fixed reimbursements, the organization has a tight margin in being able to add technology costs to an admission without being able to create a demonstrable quality change to justify the new investments.

The thoughtful CFO has a good understanding of the organization and its areas of highest value. He or she must be able to consider the organization as a whole, as well as the many pieces that make up the sum of the organizational parts. Understanding the departmental elements and the component technologies within or available to a department will assist in the overall planning and prioritization of system technologies. Technology implementation in healthcare is not a matter of whether to implement or not but is really a question of when to implement relative to other needs of the company as a whole. The implementation of a picture archiving and communications system (PACS) may have some value related to the radiology department itself but does not have the same level of contribution margin to the organization until the rest of the organization has in place the infrastructure to be able to move those images around the hospital's network. The infrastructure must support delivering those images to the providers on workstations far removed from the radiology suite or "reading room."

As the value equation can be a daunting formula to create, measurement is a necessary tool in creating a value management assessment prior to systems' acquisition, as well as ongoing after the systems have been implemented. Many, if not most organizations, lack good workflow analytics on their staff prior to systems' implementation and fewer still have the commitment to continue on with those measures after the system has been completely installed and stabilized. These are very important parts of the planning and execution process of health IT. Measurement is important to determine the baseline work units that are being consumed and to help understand the elements of the new system design that are meant to impact those individuals' productivity. The implementation of automation is a technologic change to a situation. In many cases, however, a technologic change is either insufficient or unnecessary, as the true change that is necessary is one of adaptation.

Adaptive change requires human change, be it to the technology that is in place or in the processes that they use to accomplish a task. Failure to verify a patient's identity prior to administration of a drug is an adaptive problem in many cases because of the assumption that the care provider knows the patient that he or she is treating. Despite this knowledge, patients are regularly misidentified by their care providers for a myriad of reasons. In nearly all cases, simply checking a wristband may have averted an error. Organizations today are looking for technologic solutions to such adaptive problems by putting in barcoded patient identifiers, medication labeling, and staff identification systems. Organizations are investing millions of dollars in this one workflow alone. Measurement and understanding of the initial problem and the impact of the technology on the change is imperative. If staff continue to fail to identify the patient using the bar-coded reader, then nothing has been gained through the technology investment.

MAINTAINING A STRATEGIC VIEW

Attention to the long-term goals of the organization is a paramount responsibility of the CFO. Frequently, the CFO has responsibility for oversight of the company's strategic plan that may span three to five years into the future, with very specific short-term tactics to achieve the longer term goals. This will necessitate the involvement of the CFO in the planning processes for the development and oversight of the IT strategic plan as well. The IT plan is meant to set overall IT strategies directly in support of the healthcare systems' business objectives, as well as the necessary infrastructure functions overall.

The corporate strategic plan, the IT plan, and the financial planning process all need to be tightly coordinated and monitored by the CFO. In many cases, it is the CFO who will be aware of the technologies and automation that operating units are considering for future purchase as part of the development of the yearly budget. These must then be coordinated with the IT budget and plan to maintain synchrony. Once again, it will become a process or prioritization that must be maintained in order to keep the IT budget manageable and ensure coordination with other planned activities.

It is at this point that it is often apparent that there will be a conflict between the best of breed requests that typically come from a department or division and the economic and analytic benefits of utilizing the integrated functions of an organizational core vendor, if there is already one in place. Many organizations have determined that there is greater value to the entire organization by giving up some enhanced best of breed functionality to have more integrated systems delivered by a single vendor. This integrated solutions approach allows for unified data structure and definitions that speed analysis as well as minimize costs associated with additional interfaces, vendor contracts, and maintenance challenges.

INTEGRATED PLANNING PROCESS

As noted previously, three particular plans must be constantly monitored and synchronized. The first is the healthcare organization's overall strategic plan. This is the overriding document for the organization that sets out the goals and objectives and how they are to be achieved. All other plans are subservient to the organizational strategic plan. The IT strategic plan is meant to have efforts that mirror the overall strategic plan with a series of tactical efforts in support of the larger goals. These tactics can be developed by IT leadership understanding the supporting technologies that are needed by the organization as a whole or they may in fact be underlying infrastructure activities that will build a platform to support the remaining efforts. Finally, there is the annual or rolling organizational budget. The budgeting process is an important interrelated activity, as IT will be creating their own budget based on the activities that are known and supported overall by the strategic plans. The surprise often comes from plans at individual department levels, as they will often include new technologies as part of their budgeting process as well. Depending on the organization's structure, technology funds may be centrally or locally managed. Regardless, a decision by a department to implement a technology will often have far-reaching implications on overall finances of the company and IT, either by directly affecting capital expenditures or by drawing from limited personnel in IT who may already be committed to larger organizational initiatives. The organizational CFO is in a unique position to be at the intersection point of these various plans. The CIO is usually closely aligned with both the IT and organizational plans but may not become aware of a departmental plan until after the budgeting process is complete, unless the CFO is diligent about maintaining coordination.

EFFECTIVE INFORMATION TECHNOLOGY GOVERNANCE AND OVERSIGHT

In an organization that has an IT governance committee, a great deal of effective decision making will be made. The governance leadership is best distributed across financial services, clinical services, overall operations, and IT leadership. Representatives of these diverse areas will have an understanding of all aspects of the healthcare organization and are uniquely suited to be able to render prioritization of the requests that are sure to outstrip the services that can be provided.

A leadership team as just described will have support from the organizational board to make decisions regarding project prioritization and investments. As the CFO is often a bridge between an IT governance committee and the organizational board of directors, there is an opportunity for delegation of responsibilities from the board to the governance committee. The advantage of such delegation is speed. So many decisions that must be made are under such tight time constraints that a board of directors cannot easily be convened to make decisions.

Leaders from across the organization working together in project prioritization create an opportunity for unified decision making and the associated consistent communication that is so very important for an organization to understand the *why* behind the decisions that are made. Additionally, the opportunity to have clinical and operational leaders together helps balance the socio-technical issues that were mentioned earlier. Not every problem is best solved with technology. This governance committee is structured to be able to discuss all aspects of the work processes and how automation may affect those processes. This is an opportunity for the clinicians to be invested in the technologies and to serve as champions for their implementation throughout the organization.

Accountability is a critical component of a governance committee. They are in a position of authority through which they can mandate that requestors effectively quantify the nature and effect of their requests and then be responsible for the delivery of those results once the technologies are put into place. Once more, we see the bridge between the technology itself and the necessary behavioral changes that must parallel the technology. Before a project is approved for scheduling, the governance committee can assure that the necessary parties to the project success are committed to the project, not just emotionally, but through a commitment of time as well.

Accountability and commitment can be reflected through the development of a sound business case or project charter. We will use those two terms interchangeably for illustrative purposes. Behind this charter needs to be an executive business lead who can demonstrate how the requested project is advancing the company goals and objectives and serve as the champion and communications lead for the work being done. It is important to note that there should be no IT projects, only organizational projects with significant IT components. The business case for any major project needs to include:

- Project Definition, Value Proposition, and Scope
- Identified Project Deliverables
- Investment Costs
  - Personnel time
  - Financial resources
- Project Timeline with Defined Milestones and Status Measures
- Change Management Requirements
- Detailed Risk Analysis
- Communications Plan
  - Outward for the staff
  - Upward for the board of directors
- Definitions of Success and Completion

Once the project has been approved and prioritized, a successful implementation is necessary. A well-developed and staffed project management office is equipped to take this on. A very detailed plan needs to be completed with specifics to your organization and not representative of a generic plan as would be provided by a vendor. This work needs to be completed in advance of the final contract signing and final cost negotiation. It is important to be accurate in the project timeline and overall budget, but at the same time it is wise to create a contingency of both time and money to ensure that inevitable surprises can be accounted for, if necessary. If not consumed, then there is the advantage of delivering a project ahead of schedule and budget, a status everyone can easily live with. Regular communication regarding the project status is important to maintain organizational focus, especially on large projects. The larger the project, the more important it is to keep that project's scope and status out in front of both the general organization and organizational executives.

Once initiated, a very large project with or without sizeable IT components now becomes a very large risk to the healthcare organization. Governance has a responsibility to stay attuned to that risk and manage the risks successfully. Since most of the risk is financial, the CFO will require measures to keep the project on budget. At times, the addition of an external quality assurance advisor or an evaluation from experts from an external perspective will be necessary. It is helpful to have intermittent evaluations throughout the life of the project. Not only will they measure the financial status of the project, they will assess the readiness of the organization to undertake the oncoming changes—not just of the project implementation, but for the life of the technologies being implemented. An additional risk associated with such large projects is the management of overall project scope. The size and complexity of these often leaves some project details a bit ambiguous at the outset. After it is initiated, minor changes in a project can be expected, but any major changes to scope and subsequent cost must be met with great scrutiny. Project sponsors and the management team are responsible for justifying the need for such changes and the methodology for absorbing any additional costs.

OPERATIONAL SOUNDNESS

In an organization lacking a CIO to oversee the IT department, the CFO has responsibility for managing a complex part of the healthcare organization's operation. The CFO is responsible for the department performing as expected, adequate staffing with both employees and contracted staff as necessary, and an effective security and privacy methodology that meets HIPAA and HITECH requirements.

Benchmarking the IT department to understand its performance is a challenge today because there are no good standard constructs of what an IT department is meant to look like. Nevertheless, it is important to be sure the department grows within the projected size for the organization's need. Typically a health IT department runs about 3% to 5% of the organizational operating budget, with some exceptions related to current project status. Attention, however, must be paid to how that budget is distributed among depreciations, staffing expenses, consultant resources, support, and product development. Organizations today are looking to build a department capable of growing the organization with judicious utilization of professional services on an as needed basis. An even balance between solution delivery and support capabilities keeps the department agile.

A department that is supporting technology is one that is going to be in constant flux. New technologies require staff who are nimble and open to new learning opportunities as technologies change. At the same time, an organization will have legacy applications that require very skilled resources that are in limited or short supply. Ensuring that you have sufficient skills to maintain business continuity is essential. Judicious utilization of consultant professional services is essential to most IT departments. They offer the opportunity to augment staff during times of peak service provision related to projects that are underway. They may also offer the opportunity to assist your staff at getting up to speed on a new technology or set of services with which they are unfamiliar. It is important to ensure that part of the engagement is to transfer knowledge to your own staff. Knowledge transfer will keep the engagements short and prevent the knowledge expert from being an expensive external resource that is difficult to disengage from the organization.

Managing security, privacy, and risk as part of IT operations is worthy of a book (or several volumes) in and of itself. The important elements to be aware of are, first, that many of the technologies being put into place are workflow enablers and data distributors. Those technologies now make it easy for data to be moved and accessed whether they are for business or nefarious purposes. In either case, federal legislation continues to raise the bar on an organization's responsibilities for tracking the access of patient and financial data and ability to report activities to patients and government entities. A second element to be aware of is that many of the technologies installed will require constant monitoring and real-time access by the vendors themselves. They, too, now have access to clinical and financial data. IT has a responsibility to be sure that its contract language, business associates agreements, access protocols, and auditing procedures are all very well thought out and implemented.

The unintentional disclosure of clinical or financial data or, for that matter, the loss of that data secondary to disaster or system failure, all equate to risk. Risk in and of itself must be managed and mitigated as part of the CFO's role. This risk is mitigated in several ways. The first effort is through a mechanism of insurance. This can be directly from a commercial insurance provider but may also be via contractual agreements directly with vendors and other suppliers by limiting exposure through an indemnification process. Risk is never going to be brought to zero and so the CFO has an important role in helping to measure the organizational tolerance for risk. The closer the risk is being driven to zero, the more cost associated with that risk mitigation. A good example of a cost-risk ratio is in the development of an organizational business continuity plan. Many organizations have data residing within a data center or two, and then within those data centers spread over several pieces of hardware or disk drives. The opportunity for a failure is real. Many organizations wrestle with how much money to invest in their business continuity planning process. The data redundancy and backup architecture costs can double quickly in an effort to reduce the risk of a catastrophic failure by mere tenths of a percentage point. The cost looks prohibitively high, but then again, a systems' failure can have a catastrophic expense.

VENDOR RELATIONSHIPS

Every healthcare organization will eventually be running one or more large projects that will require a heavy dependency on a vendor. At times, this dependency will be directly with the vendor supplying the software or technology and, at other times, there will be a need for additional experienced professional services via a third party. Managing the vendor relationship is a very important role for IT. A relationship between the IT leadership and the vendor leadership helps to establish a level of personal accountability that will benefit both parties. In choosing a product or professional service, past experiences can often be an important indicator of future experiences as well. Personal experience or the experience of others can be gathered to assist you in this decision making. Consortia like Premier,[1] University Health System Consortium,[2] or the Advisory Board[3] can all provide contact information for other like organizations to draw upon for vendor references.

During the contract negotiation process, it helps to stay attuned to statements of assurance that you can include within the contract. When the vendors make promises to deliver potential values or clearly defined success measures, ask them if they will be willing to go at risk as part of their contract negotiation. Asking them to accept this additional "skin" in the game makes success an equal priority for both parties. Likewise, if there is an opportunity for financial reward if measures are achieved, it may be of mutual benefit to allow the vendor to share in those rewards as well.

Projects of substantial size and visibility in the organization will warrant regular reporting to governance groups at various levels. If there are substantial vendor partners involved in the project, then it is appropriate to invite a leader from that vendor to regularly take part in any of the governance meetings. This level of participation will help keep the vendor accountable for their side of the project work and allow them to directly address any issues or concerns that the project governors may bring up.

PROJECT MANAGEMENT

Many large healthcare organizations have project management skills that excel in two areas: managing large construction projects and managing large IT implementations. With each new project, it is imperative to determine whether the necessary skill for project oversight is one that requires knowledge of the project domain (i.e., a large EHR initiative) or overall project management skills in general. Making a determination of whether this is available internally is a critical first step of project implementation.

As many current projects are multi-year EHR-related initiatives, stability in the project team will be important for project continuity and success. Mitigating the risk of staff turnover needs to be considered and addressed from the outset. Considering a solid training program with careful succession planning is a must. Some organizations will have milestone bonuses and project completion bonuses as an incentive for staff members to remain committed to a project, especially near the end when future career opportunities may become somewhat unclear.

Of equal importance to team education and commitment are the training and commitment of the staff that will be ultimately responsible for the utilization of the technologies that are to be put into place. The project will be best served to invest in two ways. The first investment is in the general training plan for the staff. Ensure that the training is timely and specific to the workflows of the users. This helps them to see the relevance of the technologies to their daily work. The second investment is in the development of super-users. These are individuals who will serve as contact points for the project development team during the design phase and then the contact point for end-users through the implementation and, finally, the stabilized phases of the project. Long term, the investment in super-users who will live at the point of contact of the technology can serve as first-line support personnel, inevitably helping to reduce the number of calls that will come into the help desk.

KEY LESSONS LEARNED

A lifetime of experience in the financial side of a healthcare organization has created many learning opportunities worth sharing and considering. Key lessons from project reporting, implementation, and post-implementation will be shared as examples of issues to watch for and methodologies for mitigating any associated risks.

Project reporting is a critical component of the communications plan of any large organizational initiative. Successful communication is necessary to mitigate unforeseen challenges to the overall project by engaging the organization in understanding the work that is before everyone. Inaccurate or incomplete project reporting can create knowledge gaps in the organization that can grow into misconceptions, rumor, or outright project failure. Reports must keep track of key progress measures and milestones and regularly report against them. In addition to the overall management of the milestones, the project reporting needs to indicate the likelihood that each key milestone will be met according to the stated plan. To the extent that a milestone may be at risk, the project management team needs to anticipate those risks and report on them so that a contingency plan may be put into place.

Implementation planning is often the most difficult milestone to be assured of. Despite the best planning and testing, there is always the risk that when the switch is pulled, something unexpected may occur. To address these situations—which do occur, it is important that the project plan include a series of mitigation or contingency steps that will be undertaken. Examples of real-life implementation crises include system level overload and associated servers crashing under the user load; successful server load balancing, but a wireless network infrastructure that is insufficient to maintain the level of traffic that is anticipated; or the possibility that the staff are not adequately prepared to handle the new workflows and processes and become woefully inefficient at their tasks, resulting in backlog and delay. The only way to mitigate against these risks is to consider as many different testing scenarios as is possible, as well as to make sure that there are resources (both technology and people) that can be on standby if they need to be recruited.

In the post-implementation window, one element is often forgotten. Projects can often be measured as successful based on the adequate and timely implementation of the desired technology and processing plans. What may often be lost is the opportunity for optimization and continued process improvement. Despite the best planning by the organization and vendor, it is likely that the vendor will not completely understand the customer and their work and at the same time, the customer will not likely be able to fully fathom the capabilities that the new technologies have to offer until after the systems have been implemented and running for a period of time. An organization can make a substantial investment only to have automated a series of inefficient or insufficient processes. Success is not just implementation; it is the achievement of the goals and objectives that were set out at the onset of the project. It will often be necessary to continue to go through a process of systems optimization to achieve and, in many cases, exceed the success measures that were initially identified.

CONCLUSION

The role of the CFO has slowly transitioned over time but has only become more complex over the years. There have been increases in the reimbursement complexity, the addition of incredible new financial systems, and most recently, the addition of even more highly complicated clinical systems. The clinical systems are necessary to support the financial and clinical decision-support processes demonstrating the value of the healthcare system relative to others. In many healthcare organizations, the addition of the CIO has helped to offload some of the CFO responsibilities, but not all. It remains a responsibility of the CFO to participate in the governance and provide oversight for the complicated IT projects and initiatives to ensure the healthcare organization's financial margin and, thus, its mission.

REFERENCES

1. Premier Insurance Management Services. http://www.premierinc.com/. Accessed November 1, 2009.

2. University HealthSystem Consortium. https://www.uhc.edu/. Accessed November 20, 2009.

3. The Advisory Board Company. http://www.advisoryboardcompany.com/. Accessed November 1, 2009.

CHAPTER 4

Follow the Money: The Revenue Cycle Story

By Miriam Paramore, FHIMSS

INTRODUCTION: FINANCIAL HEALTH INFORMATION

In the healthcare business, the point is the "care," plain and simple. However, every point of care creates a textured and complicated trajectory of financial and administrative business processes between the various stakeholders involved in that care—patients, providers and insurance companies. These business processes require specific data be transmitted between the stakeholders. When those data are conveyed and interpreted between parties with ease, not only do the business processes function better, the entire system is enhanced, care is provided more efficiently and effectively, and providers are compensated sooner. Financial health IT keeps the processes flowing and allows us to get from here to "care."

Like cars traveling a well-paved highway system, data trek from one point to the next via financial health IT, as shown in Figure 4-1. The on-ramp for the journey is the point at which a patient initiates an 'encounter' with a healthcare provider and subsequently sparks business processes and generates data to be conveyed. The conclusion of the patient's encounter serves as the exit—the end of the journey. From the providers' perspective, this beginning-to-end process is commonly referred to as the *revenue cycle*, (see Figure 4-1) while insurance companies might call it *claims processing and payment distribution*. Financial health IT keeps the revenue and payment cycles moving, as it collects necessary patient information; verifies health insurance coverage and benefit options; and facilitates the payables and receivables processes, ensuring payers (namely insurance companies) and patients who bear payment responsibility compensate providers accordingly.

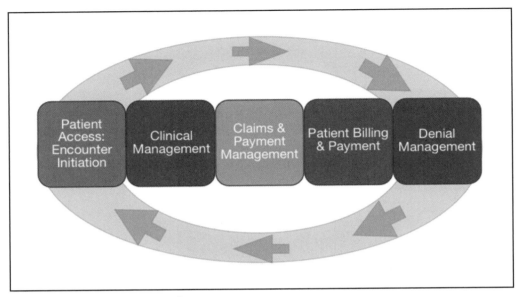

Figure 4-1: The Revenue Cycle

THE IMPORTANCE OF FINANCIAL HEALTH INFORMATION

Financial health information is the lifeblood of the healthcare industry and the exchange layer by which the information is conveyed as the most mature and highly functioning electronic system in healthcare. The usefulness of this information and the automated conveyance of it can serve as a foundation for further automation for the industry. Adoption of paperless processes throughout the industry will aid in creating a sustainable healthcare marketplace long term.

Because financial health IT keeps money and administrative data flowing, it is not commonly recognized for its potential compatibility with clinical information. Today, there is much buzz about converting paper-based PHRs into data that are electronically stored and conveyed—EHRs. Propelled by advocacy at the industry, state, and federal levels, expanding technologies and day-to-day practicality, EHRs are becoming increasingly possible and prevalent. There are many challenges moving forward with the conversion, such as privacy issues, required capital investments, and disparate technologic capabilities of involved parties, as well as the real elephant in the room: standardization of data. Nonetheless, the long-term benefits are clear, and it seems the collective consciousness is embracing the need to move forward.

The great news is that the technologic 'highway system' in use for financial and administrative data is ready and able to accommodate clinical information, too. The financial side of the healthcare industry began the transition from paper claims to electronic claims data back in the late 1980s (with advancements such as practice management software and electronic claims processing), so this information highway is paved with nearly three decades of development. Operating within mandated standardization per the Health Insurance Portability and Accountability Act (HIPAA) of 1996, the system provides secure, reliable, and efficient automation for everything from verification of insurance coverage and adjudication of claims to transmittal of remittance advice and receipt of payment. Certainly, the same capabilities can translate for EHRs as part of a nationwide health information network (NHIN) as well. By converging financial health and clinical information through this shared technology, efficiency and transparency for the entire healthcare system would be dramatically enhanced.

However, in spite of the potential impact financial health IT may have on the clinical automation yet to come, need for improvement still exists on the business side of the industry. Even after nearly 30 years, the adoption of electronic-based business practices is not 100%; paper still dominates in many areas (see Figure 4-2). Statistics from the U.S. Healthcare Efficiency Index[1] (http://www.ushealthcareindex.com/) confirm this fact. The index tracks current business inefficiencies and estimates the monetary value of those shortcomings, as well as the potential savings that would be incurred should the transition from paper to automation be completed. Frequently updated with information from an array of industry sources, the index cites some surprising figures (see Figure 4-3) that relate the importance and urgency of the paperless evolution. Most notably, upwards of $30 billion would be saved each year if participants in healthcare's business processes were to fully automate.

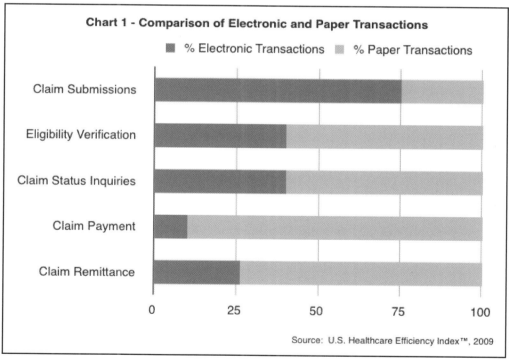

Figure 4-2: Chart 1 – Comparison of Electronic and Paper Transactions

FINANCIAL HEALTH INFORMATION SYSTEMS BY SETTING

Anyone involved in the healthcare system is a participant in and a recipient of financial health information. From the patient presenting an insurance card and the frontline staff member who receives it, to the practitioner who makes notes about rendered care that allow the accounting representative to submit details to the insurance company, every person is party to the creation and conveyance of financial health information.

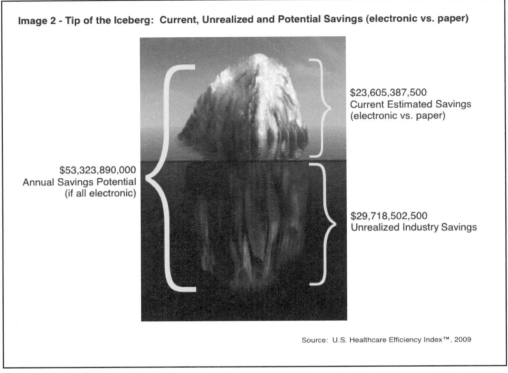

Image 2 - Tip of the Iceberg: Current, Unrealized and Potential Savings (electronic vs. paper)

$23,605,387,500
Current Estimated Savings
(electronic vs. paper)

$53,323,890,000
Annual Savings Potential
(if all electronic)

$29,718,502,500
Unrealized Industry Savings

Source: U.S. Healthcare Efficiency Index™, 2009

Figure 4-3: Image 2 – Tip of the Iceberg: Current, Unrealized and Potential Savings (electronic versus paper)

With a quick survey of the typical revenue cycle, the roles of the various players come to light as depicted in Figure 4-4. Healthcare providers take in information from patients and, in turn, send out information to payers to receive compensation for care rendered. Similarly, pharmacies fill prescriptions and also convey pertinent data to payers. Payers receive data to make determinations about coverage and payments and, likewise, offer information to explain benefits to patients and caregivers. Consumers of healthcare—patients—navigate the system to make sense of it all, from benefits and eligibility to financial responsibility and payment alternatives. Today, as our healthcare system shifts to a consumer model, patients are more integrally involved in payment than ever before, heightening the need for open exchange of digestible, transparent information from beginning to end of the revenue cycle.

Beyond these commonly identified players, there is a layer in the healthcare system that many who are not in the business are unaware exists: *healthcare information intermediaries*. Sometimes referred to as *clearinghouses*, these intermediaries are companies that facilitate the transmittance of data between parties in the revenue cycle. They actually built the aforementioned technologic highway system that the entire healthcare industry benefits from today. As informational arbitrators, clearinghouses provide solutions for translating data for universal recognition and integrating necessary technologies and systems, and they serve as the conduits for billing and payments. These companies must be responsive to changes in the industry—keeping watch on everything from passage of relevant legislation and development of technologic advancements to introduction of updated HIPAA transaction standards and code sets—to create and implement responsive solutions that apply across the board. Clearinghouses are *covered entities* under HIPAA, meaning they must adhere to all privacy and security rules.

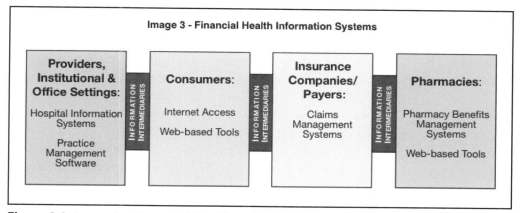

Figure 4-4: Image 3 – Financial Health Information Systems

Technology allows all participants to handle business processes and related data transmittance more fluidly. Interconnectivity is the key for progressing toward the increased efficiency and transparency of a fully automated system. Automation is more important than ever in light of spiraling medical costs and the evolving consumer model of healthcare.

With so many players in the industry, it is no small feat to keep up with the nuances and business needs of each area. Following is an overview of the various settings as they relate to financial health information, to serve as a roadmap for the many points of interest involved with points of care.

PROVIDER SETTING: INSTITUTIONAL

Hospitals, health systems with multiple locations or practices comprised of 15 or more physicians, are defined as *institutions* within the context of financial health information. Obviously, the larger a provider setting, the more resources it likely has. Thus, institutions often possess the capital and capacity to introduce and maintain technologies that some smaller providers take longer to adopt. The progression of financial health information automation in institutions is illustrative of the many phases and trends throughout the entire healthcare system.

Today, institutions rely on data transfer throughout the revenue cycle much as they began to do so in the late 1980s into the 1990s. Electronic claims processing led to electronic remittance advice, the electronic equivalent of the explanation of benefits (EOB) that burgeoned to automated eligibility verifications. Those areas are still the anchor components of electronic financial health information. However, the types and nature of the available data have become more voluminous and complex as technological advancements have widened the information highway with increased capabilities and capacity. Likewise, how those technologies are accessed has also advanced.

Presently, providers access automation online, with the input of secure log-in information on Web-based systems. Clearinghouses are able to provide updates en masse to institutions' systems automatically and remotely for immediate, seamless operation—a far cry from the on-location modem installing and program loading and updating that was required in previous decades. Likewise, today's accounting and patient information systems are also typically Web-based and markedly improved from the early incarnations of system software, contributing to improved workflow all around. And the data and transactions these systems are interchanging are now standardized by HIPAA (though subject to interpretation by individual payers), unlike the wide-ranging, non-standard information of past generations.

Even as technology continues to advance, institutions face old and new challenges. Hospitals often have three to five systems of varying architecture that must be interoperable; normalizing these systems is essential to improving workflow. As medical records transition from paper to electronic, information in those records is disparate, and solutions must be created to effectively push or pull uniform data out. According to the U.S. Healthcare Efficiency Index,[1] upwards of 90% of payments are still processed in labor intensive, slow-to-post paper form, as institutions are challenged to process standard payment transactions.

Financial health IT is the ultimate tool for institutions (and payers), as it not only enables the creation and integration of solutions to the aforementioned hurdles to automation, it is already configured to address other notable shifts occurring in the healthcare industry. For example, consumerism has quickly come to the forefront, and financial health IT is offering innovative options to help patients pay. In the past, institutions relied almost solely on revenue paid by insurance companies and, thus, operated within systems that focused on data interchange with major payers. Today, providers must deal with patients directly in the payment process; therefore, the industry is highly motivated to expand capabilities for effectively communicating with consumer patients regarding projected costs and alternatives for payments.

As a matter of fact, many institutions are revisiting their approaches to staffing the frontline of patient access. Formerly, frontline positions were often relegated to being purely administrative because the related tasks (scheduling, verifying, and completing registration information) were rather mundane, and with automated financial health information capture and processing, the effort to input data was minimal. In the evolution to healthcare consumerism, the point of entry is more pivotal; it is a uniquely teachable moment, in which an admissions representative can assess a patient's coverage, offer insights about anticipated costs and coverage options, and provide preemptive payment planning.

To that end, institutions are relying on technology to make financial health information transparent. Transparency enables institutions to educate patients in all aspects of the costs of their care, from the moment of *patient access* (when patients enter the system by initiating an encounter with a healthcare provider) until they exit the system after care is rendered. It is essential that institutions remove the veil between patients and processes, so that proper expectations are set and consumers are never left financially blindsided or unprepared for payment responsibility.

Financial health IT is already addressing the more complex needs of the consumer healthcare model by heightening transparency and incorporating more consumer-friendly options. Payment responsibility estimators allow institutions to advise patients about anticipated costs, and advancements in EOBs are also providing more pertinent, easier-to-review information. Additionally, expanded modes of payment are being introduced to allow consumers to pay online or by phone, with credit card or direct withdrawal.

PROVIDER SETTING: OFFICE

Other providers cover a gamut of shapes and sizes, including private practices, small physician offices (one to fourteen physicians), walk-in clinics, physical therapy practices, home care and skilled nursing. Even labs, durable medical equipment providers, and ancillary services such as transportation to and from appointments as provided by Medicaid, fall into this all-encompassing category. Roughly 65% of care delivered in this segment occurs in office settings, and more than 50% of those offices are staffed by just one or two physicians.

Adoption of financial health IT has historically been slower for smaller offices constrained by staffing, budgetary and data standardization issues. However, today, these providers are increasingly motivated by cost savings and efficiencies to go paperless. Automation alleviates workload for employees, makes practices easier to manage, and streamlines the process of getting paid. It also saves money. A 2006 Milliman study showed that a fully-loaded electronic system could reduce a practice's yearly insurance administration costs by more than $42 per physician, tallying a savings of $3.73 per claim for providers.[2] Additionally, a report from America's Health Insurance Plans (AHIP)[3] from the same year indicated that 98% of electronically filed claims process within 30 days, markedly less than the processing time for manual claims. Small office and tertiary providers are more heavily reliant on the services of clearinghouses to mediate information exchange and achieve these savings and efficiencies (compared with institutional providers that often have resources to customize their own systems and solutions).[3]

Ironically, small offices create approximately 90% of the claims volume in the healthcare system, yet only about 10% of total charges, the inverse of institutional statistics. Because every patient encounter or office visit must be filed separately, small office claims volume is very high, while the charges associated with such visits are typically contained. Conversely, once a patient enters an institutional healthcare facility (i.e., a hospital), all subsequent care and related charges incurred until point of discharge are documented on a single claim.

This extremely large claim volume for smaller offices made adoption of electronic methods for claim filing and adjudication a must because it minimizes the potential for error. Even still, 8% to 10% of claims filed through electronic data interchange (EDI) are rejected back to the provider from the payer due to improper input (i.e., invalid insurance information, incomplete or incorrect patient information, redundant filing, etc.) on the provider side. The information intermediaries—clearinghouses—are contacted to identify and resolve such problems, though the error rests with the providers that originated the claims. However, proper use of financial health IT may not only lessen risk of errors overall, it holds the potential to make the entire process more transparent, so that payers and providers can see for themselves what happens when claims are rejected by making information accessible to all involved parties.

The benefits of transparency extend beyond revealing claims' adjudication issues or aiding in consumer payment responsibilities, as previously described. Transparency, as facilitated through financial health information, has the potential to lead to clinical trends assessments, networking and information sharing for physician practices and within specialties. Because clearinghouses have relationships with literally hundreds of thousands of providers and thousands of payers, they likewise have potential access to untold volumes of useful clinical data. Great opportunities exist to transform those data into useable information via the existing information highway—collectively enlightening a sometimes fractured national network of small providers on ways to improve quality and efficiency of care for better patient outcomes. (Of course, payers also have access to such data and have long attempted similar reporting, but those attempts have often been perceived as biased. Data from neutral clearinghouses may be more readily accepted and interpreted.)

As close as that potential transparency is, there are obstacles on the information highway. Standardization and normalization of data is still a stumbling block. Clearinghouses offer some methods for converging disparate data and systems with accommodations for security and privacy, but not every provider is adopting all the technology.

Another technology that provider offices are slowly adopting is electronic funds transfer (EFT). Presently, only 20% to 25% of remittances for this provider type are transmitted electronically, and of those, even fewer—just 8%—are paid by EFT. The rest are processed with software that allows the office to print checks related to ERAs. Clearly, this side of the industry strongly prefers to process paper checks to finalize payments. However, some payers such as Medicare have begun requiring EFT, and others are motivating the transition by offering better terms for electronic transactions. Certainly, this trend will continue. Already many physicians' offices are acknowledging the value that EFTs provide in terms of time savings and efficiencies.

CONSUMER SETTING

As mentioned, today's healthcare system is shifting to a consumer model, in which care must be addressed from a more retail perspective. As patients become payers alongside their insurance carriers or other paying entities, such as Medicare and Medicaid, they need access to detailed information regarding costs of care as well as payment alternatives unlike ever before.

The role of financial health IT is pivotal in this shifting model. Historically, neither payers nor providers have had to interact in such detail with patients on matters of cost and direct payment. Today's system of co-insurance, consumer incentives, tax advantaged plans of healthcare savings and spending accounts, and retail models is a far cry from the full indemnity insurance of the 1970s and 1980s or the health maintenance organizations (HMOs) and preferred provider organizations (PPOs) that became prevalent in the 1990s and carried us into the new century. These past models in large part circumvented patients when it came time for cost break-outs and payment.

Generally speaking, payers and providers are simply not equipped or attuned to deal directly with consumers. Yet with tools created by clearinghouses and made accessible on the existing information highway, these entities are positioned to usher in this new era.

And usher it in they must. Healthcare inflation has grown at an unsustainable rate, thus precipitating the need to create econometrics for consumers to use healthcare more intelligently. The consumer model is purposed in creating more knowledgeable patients who prioritize well care, prevention, and ongoing health maintenance in an effort to stave off chronic diseases, avoid the need for costly emergency department visits, etc. For this system to achieve its fullest potential, financial and administrative data must ultimately converge with clinical data, so that patients, providers, and payers make the most informed decisions.

The financial information component is already providing traction for the new consumerism. Providers have begun to use existing and newly available tools to guide patients through the system, from initiation of an encounter to the final payment for services rendered. From moment one, patients must be fully informed about the insurance and benefits available to them. Providers must estimate expected treatment, and then, using contractual allowances established with third-party payers, also estimate the anticipated financial responsibility of the patient. At this point, alternatives for supplemental coverage can be explored as well. (It is important to note that availability of coverage does not typically equate to treatment limitations; medical facilities will provide care in accordance with their stated mission, regardless of payment capabilities.)

Providers must bill and reconcile payment very accurately with retail-like information, options, and attention to detail. There are large administrative costs involved with handling consumer payments for providers, especially hospitals that must deal with lock boxes, banking, and financial vehicles. The goal of a payment solution program is to electronically enable healthcare providers in receiving payment as soon as reasonably possible following a patient encounter along with any third-party insurance payments. Healthcare providers endeavor to both reduce consumer write-off (bad debt) and increase their cash flow, all the while facilitating as many payment options as possible for ease of consumers' use. From the provider perspective, there is reduced administrative overhead in receiving and reconciling payments electronically in their system. Providing multiple options that are within a consolidated platform affords them a comprehensive collection solution for all modalities, whether the payment is received over the telephone, online, or via paper payment.

The new model is compelling all providers to make accommodations for more consumer-oriented payment alternatives, such as acceptance of pre-payments and online payments supported by real-time access to information via the Internet. Though there are initial investments to incorporate these options, the expenditures outweigh the risk of losing 3% to 5% of revenue through mishandling. Services and systems offered by clearinghouses allow providers to manage the system effectively.

Long term, the data collected on the financial health information highway will be very helpful in assessing the efficacy of the consumer model. By converging financial and administrative data with clinical information, patient/consumer behavior can be analyzed and reviewed to assess success. Web-based tools will further engage consumers in the healthcare process, accommodating a more interactive, integrated approach to healthcare.

PHARMACY SETTING

Pharmacy services have been ahead of the rest of the healthcare system in terms of electronic integration. Compliance with standards for pharmacy/prescription electronic data interchange (EDI), created more than 15 years ago, was directly tied to reimbursements, hence the early motivation toward integration. The introduction of pharmacy benefits management (PBM) organizations also aided in establishing EDI early on. With such an established, strong foundation, today's pharmacies enjoy real-time, standardized transactions and are readily welcoming advanced technologic capabilities, such as e-prescribing.

E-prescribing is the modern alternative to the scribbled notations on small prescription pads. Not surprisingly, those often illegible, easily misplaced, written prescriptions that prevailed in the healthcare system have led to measurable errors in interpretation and related patient care issues over the years. Electronically submitted prescriptions are clearly stated and automatically transmitted, thus greatly reducing or altogether eliminating misreads and human error. Additionally, an electronic prescribing system is able to automatically issue drug formulary alerts. Unfortunately, many e-prescribing systems do not yet handle cancellations or alterations very effectively.

The American Medical Association's online *AMedNews* reported a pilot program at Detroit's Henry Ford Health System experienced more than 50,000 such alerts out of more than half a million e-prescriptions in less than three years' time.[4] To encourage e-prescribing, the government has instituted a program by which reimbursements are enhanced for parties that employ electronic prescriptions. Such automation leads to easier, better managed work flows, resulting in cost savings and efficiencies that translate across the board.

Recent programs and studies have shone a spotlight on the undeniable, integral impact that proper prescription and drug compliance have on the entire healthcare system. A 2007 report by the National Council on Patient Information and Education calculated that non-adherence to prescriptions cost the U.S. healthcare system approximately $100 billion annually, with $47 million of that cost attributed to drug-related hospitalization.[5] Clearly, proper adherence actually reduces overall healthcare costs. When patients comply with the prescribed parameters of their medications, they remain healthier and ultimately require fewer physician encounters and treatments. Medicare Part D, which provides prescription coverage for previously uncovered individuals, has also done its part to reduce the need for encounters in the healthcare system. The increasingly electronic system is already bearing fruit, yet more must be done.

Adherence programs are being enhanced and/or developed by converging financial and administrative data with clinical and drug adherence information. By carefully assessing this converged information, gleaned by clearinghouses, physicians may be informed when patients fail to fill prescriptions or fail to refill them according to orders. Healthcare providers, in accordance with patient allowances for data sharing, may be given opportunities to advise and guide patients to comply with prescriptions, simply by knowing when they have failed or been unable to do so previously.

Statistics reveal the immense need to address prescription compliance. In spite of the aforementioned successes, prescriptions continue to be commonly disregarded, improperly taken, and infrequently refilled. Only 50% to 70% of every 100 prescriptions issued are taken to the pharmacy to be filled, and of those, only 48% to 66% are picked up. Furthermore, the majority of prescriptions, 70% to 75%, are taken improperly, while 80% to 85% are not refilled as prescribed.[6]

As the facilitators, transmitters, and repositories of useful data, clearinghouses can potentially help providers and pharmacists manage prescriptions at a very advanced, clinically-based level. The potential exists to funnel prescription information through an evaluation process to ensure proper dispensing occurs. This system catches errors and abuses, redundancies, non-compliance issues, and can even assist in determining alternative medications and illuminating potential drug interaction issues. While this effective system involves only one payer, the technology exists to translate this approach for multiple payers and pharmacies.

As technologies advance and information becomes more available, the pharmacy industry is shifting toward a proactive informatics track in which better data lead to better patient outcomes, as well as reduced costs. Drug dispensing is becoming automated, thus freeing up pharmacists to adopt clinical approaches. Today's pharmacists are delving more fully into informatics to provide thorough consultations and advice to patients.

INTEROPERABILITY

As just discussed, patients' adherence to prescriptions can ultimately affect the overall health of the population, which, in turn, can impact the healthcare system through fewer encounters in clinical settings, visits to Emergency Departments, etc. Every aspect of the system is affected by the others, like cars on the highway. If a lead car brakes, the others behind observe the brake lights and follow suit by slowing to avoid collision.

Likewise, all types of financial health information are linked through interoperable systems that are ever sharing and receiving data that guide the flow of the revenue cycle. For the flow to go smoothly, there must be 'rules of the road' on the information highway—applied standards and code sets to normalize or make compatible the content and format of the data traveling back and forth. These standards serve as the mechanisms that allow information to be conveyed predominantly between providers and payers, often through the interpretative assistance of information intermediaries. HIPAA, including its subsequent modifications, is the primary source of rules for the transaction standards and code sets that ensure financial health information's interoperability. This public law was purposed in providing administrative simplification to best deal with electronic information, while also ensuring the protection and privacy of it.

In terms of volume of 'traffic' on the information highway, payers represent the majority, and thus, they strongly affect the flow for the entire revenue cycle. For example, because HIPAA made allowances for payers to create propriety interpretations of certain transaction standards and code sets (communicated in payer "companion guides"), the entire industry is impacted by the varying criteria set forth from payer to payer. Providers are constantly challenged to make sense of varying codes, as they must interpret payers' companion guides and reconcile differing versions of electronic remittance advice (ERA). In the highway analogy, it is as if payers all must acknowledge a speed limit, though they are able to individually determine their preferred paces. Obviously, the inconsistencies make traveling the information highway more challenging for the other entities using the roadway.

At present, the industry—already functioning under near-crushing inflation and demands to improve efficiencies—is facing decisions about HIPAA 5010 that would forcibly compel payers to adhere to a single set of standards and code sets (versus the proprietary, interpretive approach currently in use). This potential shift would involve major upfront investments, as systems industry wide would need to be altered or built anew and operational procedures would be forever revamped. Yet the benefits of universally employed standards merit the investment and effort. Not only would clinical and administrative data flow more efficiently, clinical information would also be more effectively integrated into such a unified, fully interoperable system.

Clearinghouses serve an essential role in adopting unified transaction standards and code sets. With immense resources in terms of technology, data stores and established interconnected relationships, clearinghouses would offer great aid in preparing, transitioning, and fully converting to a singular system. The outcome of this HIPAA change would impact the entire healthcare system, but most immediately, it would affect the financial health information sector charged with implementation.

PROTECTION OF FINANCIAL HEALTH INFORMATION

No matter what happens regarding the normalization of transaction standards and code sets, protection and privacy of financial health information (and all medical records, for that matter) remain essential, primary priorities for all parties involved. Just as technology paved the way for efficient flow of information, it also created an opportunity for that information to be compromised. Responsively, the government, through the Department of HHS' Office for Civil Rights, has legislated and payers and providers have invested in measures and mechanisms to assure the security of information and the privacy and rights of patients. Indeed, the same law that addresses health information "portability" equally addresses the system's "accountability" with that information as well.

Payers (referred to as "health plans" in HIPAA language), healthcare providers, and clearinghouses are all covered entities of the rules and statutes of HIPAA, and additional provisions have been instituted for small payers, providers, and other small businesses. All covered entities are bound to comply with the Privacy Rule, which establishes the baseline of protections of privacy and individual rights related to electronic exchange of health information.

The Privacy Rule asserts required guidelines regarding transparency and openness, so that individuals are aware of all policies, procedures, and technology that affect their health information. To that end, covered entities must make known their methods for collection and use of information. With proper opportunity and knowledge, individuals are assured the right to make informed decisions about the collection, conveyance, and use of their health information.

Covered entities must safeguard information through "reasonable" measures of administrative, technical, and physical security. The rule does not address specific requirements for safeguarding, as these details will inevitably vary from entity to entity based on size and nature of business and practices. Nonetheless, the implementation of security measures is essential and must be integrated into operations from moment one for any and all electronic financial health information transactions.

CHALLENGES OF AUTOMATION

The healthcare industry is historically slow to adopt operational technology. This seems contrary to the image often held by the public. We revere the medical industry for developing new and seemingly miraculous advancements in diagnostic technologies on a regular basis. How can the industry that saves lives, develops ways to heal, and discovers cures lag behind in technology? Why can consumers bank online and check themselves in at airports, yet still only have limited access to EMRs?

The reality is the healthcare industry is extremely complex. The nature of medical care, with its nuances, unpredictable complications, and individual iterations, is tangled in multi-layered issues of privacy and security and draped in exorbitant costs and complex payment structures that evolve almost ceaselessly. Related transactions, which may literally be life-or-death in nature on some occasions, are rarely uniform. Incorporating technology is the right thing to do for healthcare, but it is also immensely daunting and difficult to implement across the board.

Certainly, the fact that payers may individually interpret transaction standards and code sets is one very surmountable problem. Likewise, standards or procedures may vary from state to state, even though working within the framework of federally mandated HIPAA rules. For automation to jive and interoperate, systems must speak the same languages or, at a minimum, be afforded adept translators. The clearinghouse industry has and continues to play a vital role in interpreting electronic information to be universally accessible, useable, and beneficial.

Presently, there is great need for an industry-wide awareness of already established alternatives for automation. Financial health information is by far the most deeply rooted, successfully operating, electronically-based system in the industry. The technological highway on which financial health information travels at the rate of nearly 13 billion transactions each year is often not in the common consciousness of some clinically-oriented professionals or regional and federal legislators and activists who are newer to the discussion. As the industry, the government, and society at large join the groundswell of support to take all of healthcare electronic, awareness must be raised regarding existing alternatives. Unifying development efforts and applying already operational, proven technologies is the surest way to accomplish industry-wide automation.

It may still be a long road to full automation, but it is certainly not a new one. The system simply needs to follow the financial health information to head in the right direction—and get to the point.

And the point is the "care."

REFERENCES

1. U.S. Healthcare Index 2009. http://www.ushealthcareindex.com/index.php. Accessed October 23, 2009.

2. Phelan J, Naugle A. *Electronic Transaction Savings*. Opportunities for Physician Practices. Milliman Inc; January 2006.

3. AHIP Report. *An Updated Survey of Health Care Claims Receipt and Processing Times*, May 2006.

4. Chin T. *Amednews.online*. (March 27, 2006). E-prescribing reduces errors, cost for large group practice. http://www.ama-assn.org/amednews/2006/03/27/bisb0327.htm. Accessed October 22, 2009.

5. National Council on Patient Information and Education. Enhancing Prescription Medicine Adherence: A National Plan, August 2007 Report. http://www.talkaboutrx.org/documents/enhancing_prescription_medicine_adherence.pdf. Accessed December 30, 2009.

6. Long D., IMS Health, National Association of Chain Drug Stores National Conference. February 2009.

CHAPTER 5

Physicians' Views on Clinical Information Technology

By Raymond A. Gensinger, Jr., MD, CPHIMS, FHIMSS

INTRODUCTION

The roles and opportunities for physicians to be leaders in healthcare have been growing steadily. Just a few decades ago, the highest ranking physicians in a large integrated delivery network (IDN) were likely to be the medical director or chief of staff for the organization. Today, physicians are found in the boardroom, the C suites, as well as in state and federal congressional seats. One of the newest "C" designations has been that of the chief medical information officer (CMIO). Today, there are several hundred CMIOs practicing in U.S. healthcare locations.

The CMIO is often a partner or direct report to the organization's CIO. Other reporting relationships for the CMIO are to the chief medical officer (CMO) or to the chief executive officer (CEO). Regardless of the reporting relationships, the CMIO typically serves in two capacities. First, the CMIO has responsibilities, in partnership with the CIO, to deliver the IT strategic plan for the organization in accordance with the overall company goals and objectives. The second, and more complicated of responsibilities, is to facilitate technology readiness and adoption among the organization's clinical staff. It is important to reiterate that the position is not exclusive to oversight of technology for the medical staff but for all clinical staff. Some organizations will divide the general oversight of IT between the clinical and business systems of the organization, with the CIO overseeing infrastructure and business systems and leaving clinical applications and activities within the CMIO's purview.

A physician or nurse could equally serve in the CMIO role for an organization. Detailed understanding of technology is not the most important underlying criteria to hold this position. What is more important is to understand the application of IT to the provision of care and its necessity to assist in the transformation of medicine from the current level of infrastructure innovation to industry innovation—the next great medical transformation. To facilitate that transformation, the CMIO must also be an influential organizational leader. In this role, the CMIO must wield considerable levels of informal authority to align and guide disparate members of the healthcare team and organization to arrive at a common clinical adoption model.

This chapter will walk the reader through the historic relationships between medicine, technology, the advancements of medical technology, the innovation transformation model, and then, finally, through a detailed example of organizational teaming to create a transformational infrastructure via an EHR selection process.

MEDICINE IS TECHNOLOGY

The application of medical sciences can be viewed as a technology of sorts. If you accept the online definition of *technology* as "the practical application of knowledge especially in a particular area,"[1] then it would follow that any practitioner engaged in the efforts to provide healthcare or health advice is, in fact, wielding technology. In the case of IT, the individual is applying his or her knowledge to development in the area of computing systems. The role of the CMIO today is to meld the knowledge of both medicine and technology into revolutionary new disciplines in the advancement of health IT.

Personal health and, essentially, longevity have long been the goals of our species. Regardless of cultural origins, there has always been a place for a medicine man or woman, healer, or shaman. The role of these individuals was typically to apply their knowledge in the return to health of their fellows. Typically, efforts were intended to avoid death. Demonstration of the practice of preventive medicine is present in the book of Leviticus and the priestly codes therein. This serves as an early reference of the connection between priests and ministers of health. The tenets and teachings of this book are examples of the earliest of medical technologies.

Figure 5-1 lists medical technologies from the last 500 years. Clearly, this is only representative of a few of the discoveries in this interval, but what is apparent is that there appears to be an oscillation back and forth between technologies that enable care providers to learn more about what is invisible to the naked eye: the discovery of the microscope, EKG, or perhaps an MRI and medical interventions that have leveraged the knowledge gained from the technology; this includes the use of antiseptics, hypertensive therapies, and noninvasive surgeries and procedures. Decades would pass between major medical milestones, while in today's world, new milestones are occurring at a breakneck speed. This cycle between discovery, intervention, analysis, and new discoveries is referred to as the *translational research cycle*, and it is getting shorter all the time.

The information technologies in healthcare have undoubtedly advanced the science, quality, and outcomes of patients. The challenge to those providing care for patients has been that the volume of medical data they are responsible for gathering, understanding, and acting upon has grown exponentially. This is just for the provision of care for a *single* patient. This does not take into account the aggregation of that same data across multiple patients and locations to provide understanding of disease at the population level. The aggregation of this population level data is critical for the understanding of disease and the effectiveness of therapies.

Microscope	1590	Pacemaker	1952
Stethoscope	1860	Space race	1960s
Antiseptics	1867	Test tube baby	1978
Vaccines	1880	First magnetic	
Aspirin	1899	resonance imaging	1980
Electrocardiogram	1910	Artificial heart	1982
Insulin	1922	Cloned sheep	1996
Penicillin	1928	Genome map	2003
		Gene Therapy	20xx

Figure 5-1: A Brief History of Medical Technology

Hospital courses are getting shorter and the number of providers as part of the inpatient care team is growing. Today, at our academic medical center, it is becoming more common for a patient to have a hospitalization of three to four days and be seen by as many as 10 or 15 physicians during that one hospitalization (assuming a primary care team, two or three specialists, and their associated physician trainees). This differs considerably from just a couple of decades ago when a primary care provider or general surgeon was likely to provide the totality of physician medical care during a hospitalization.

Many organizations are moving to EHRs, but there are many more yet to go. Various reports indicate that, currently, the adoption rate for EHRs in U.S. hospitals falls somewhere between 2% to 8%, depending on whether you are looking at comprehensive or partially implemented systems, respectively. That means that as many as 90% of U.S. hospitals may still be trying to manage effective patient care utilizing paper-based documentation and reporting systems. Consider that a typical four-day stay is likely to yield more than 100 pages of new documentation, and patients with some chronic diseases, such as heart failure or renal failure, may have multiple admissions in a year. It will not take long before the historic record of information grows too deep for the next care provider to be able to synthesize the totality of the patient's condition history effectively using manual processes alone.

The application of medical IT is the only possible solution to the accumulation of an insurmountable volume of patient medical record information. Clinicians will require the EHR tools to be able to aggregate and filter the medical information, so that it can be reviewed in digestible, provider-relevant components. Department operational staff will utilize decision support and data aggregation tools to monitor and track patient quality and safety measures. Hospital administration will utilize business performance metrics and operational dashboards to measure their hospital effectiveness against internal targets and local and national benchmarks.

TECHNOLOGY AS A TOOL

It is human nature to design and manufacture tools in an effort to ease our labors. This skill is what differentiates us from so many other animal species. Interestingly, we often approach problems that we face as typically those of a technical nature; thus, we look for technologic solutions to those problems. As noted by Heifetz and Linsky,[2,p13] technical problems "…are not amenable to authoritative expertise or standard operating procedures…we call these adaptive challenges because they require experiments… sustainability of change depends on having the people with the problem internalize the change itself."[2,p13] Problems in medicine need to be addressed, considering both the technical and adaptive nature of the problems that they present. In many cases, we need more than tools; we need the willingness to change.

Computer technology has been a tool of medicine coming of age in the 1960s with the utilization of monitoring, transmission, and recording of astronaut vital sign information as part of the Gemini and Apollo missions. Attending to and managing the stresses of astronauts 250,000 miles from the nearest physician was the true initiation of telemedicine. This is an appropriate technical fix to a problem of recording medical information from such great distances.

In today's healthcare environment, we look to technology to solve nearly every problem that we are facing. This has had a series of unintended consequences to which we need to pay attention. The first consequence of importance has to do with the development of best-of-breed product solutions. Enterprising clinicians and computing companies were quick to hone in on areas of frustration and data management challenges. Hence, we began to see the development of specialty applications for both the practice management and, eventually, the clinical sides of medicine. Business systems in support of registration, scheduling, billing, and collection were developed early on by large mainframe computer companies. Other companies began to develop clinical tools to support the radiology departments with radiology information systems (RIS) and PACS, as well as systems for laboratory, pharmacy, and operating room purposes. The consequence of these developments—best-of-breed solutions, has been that hospitals have highly effective systems that serve single purposes and do very little to bridge the care of patients from location to location within the hospital. In essence, the systems lack *interoperability*, the ability to exchange data and make use of the exchanged data, and they often lack *integration*, the ability to simply exchange data, as well.

A second unintended consequence of the implementation of IT was the failure to truly understand the problems that were meant to be resolved. Essentially the trouble was failing to note that the problem at hand was one of an adaptive nature, rather than one of a true technical nature. An example of this in the current day is the process of medication reconciliation. Providers are expected to review the current medications a patient is taking prior to a medical visit and reconcile that list with the medications that are to be continued following the visit, thus reconciling the patient's before- and after-medication plan. The reconciled list then becomes the reference point for the patient and provider at the next visit. Vendor after vendor has gone about the approach of trying to develop a technology to facilitate the process of medication reconciliation. However, no solution has met with satisfactory acceptance. The reason for this failure has very little to do with the effectiveness of the technologies as developed by the vendors, but has everything to do with the adaptive nature of the problem. As Heifetz and Linsky note, "By trying to solve adaptive challenges for people, at best you will reconfigure it as a technical problem and create some short-term relief."[2,p123] This is also known as a *socio-technical problem.*

For medication reconciliation to work, be it on paper or within an EHR, there needs to be invested clinicians and patients who value the results of the work they are doing. The system is not capable of resolving the problem itself. Human input is required because the systems are incapable of accurately determining whether the patient has filled the prescriptions written, determining whether medications have been taken as prescribed, or assessing if a external provider has altered the medication plan. Medication reconciliation is a socio-technical problem that requires an adaptive solution, a person or persons invested in effectively tracking the patient's medication history.

HEALTHCARE TRANSFORMATION

The history of healthcare reform extends back to the early part of the 20th century when first efforts were made by President Teddy Roosevelt's Progressive party to call for the establishment of social insurance. Most recent memory is littered with the failed attempts of reform as sponsored by health plans themselves with the introduction of managed care and then by the notable failure of the Clinton administration to undertake reform in the 1990s. Now, all eyes are on healthcare reform as proposed by the Obama administration and acted upon by the U.S. Congress. While the details and approaches of the plans are still being wrestled, it will likely be reshaped in several ways. In the plan, there will be a flavor of universal healthcare coverage, payment reforms, and an opportunity for tort reform. Also, payments will become dependent upon the demonstrated meaningful use of health IT centered around EHRs.

The pace of change in healthcare is dramatic. Historically, change had been very slow following an evolutionary approach. Evolution, much like a glacier, moves so slowly that change is unperceivable. Today's pace can be more likened to a NASCAR race. We are moving at nearly 200 mph, but we seem to be going in circles and not really getting anywhere new. The destination we are trying to reach, as clinicians for our patients, is higher quality of care. We want to see better outcomes for our patients at lower or, at least, the same cost. The criticism, of course, is that the costs of healthcare in the United States are out of control, and we do not have the outcomes to justify these incredible costs. We blame a great deal of the cost on the inefficiencies of the American healthcare system, as a result of the inappropriate use of diagnostic tests, repeating those tests when the results are not found or believed, and the myriad of inefficiencies and added costs of complications associated with a medical record tracking system that essentially has not changed for more than a hundred years, pen to paper.

The system is so complex and so interconnected that any efforts to change one element of the system are likely to have a cascading effect throughout all other segments of the healthcare process. As Kotter[3] has pointed out, this is often a source of transformation failure. One change in and of itself is not destined to fail; rather, we fail to take into account the interconnectedness of systems and the effects that one change causes to the whole system.

If we look at Figure 5-2, we see the representation of an innovation or maturation "S curve." Along the *x* axis, we have time represented in quarters for simplicity. The *y* axis is meant to be representative of innovation or maturation. How well the classic healthcare organization has utilized the capability that its technologies offer can be represented by one of the two lines. The straight gray line represents the organization that continues to invest in new technologies, yet fails to leverage that technology to its fullest capacity. The curve that looks like the *S* curve is representative of the organization that has identified the capabilities technology offers and has matured in its care delivery models to fully take advantage of the capability. The difference between the two lines is the opportunity gap that exists between the maturation and utilization.

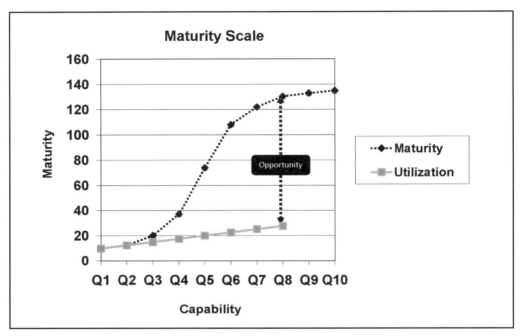

Figure 5-2: Organizational Maturation Scale

Lacking competition, a single healthcare organization in a community can survive, utilizing the line that slowly elevates. In a highly competitive healthcare marketplace, however, each of the organizations must follow the opportunities of the innovation the *S* curve represents. Coffman and Kaufman[4] nicely explain the concept of innovation and transformation (as developed by Kirsten Moy and Greg Ratliff[5]) in *Innovation and Transformation: A Lifecycle Model.*[4] A competitive healthcare organization has mastered the first *S* curve of product innovation and the second *S* curve of infrastructure innovation. We are awaiting the first healthcare organization to make the final *S* curve transformation—that of *Industry Innovation.*

Figure 5-3 is adapted from Moy and Ratliff[5] to demonstrate the transformation to Industry Innovation. The boxes labeled *1* and *2* are indicative of the two periods in time when an industry, in this case healthcare, must make the leap from one *S* curve to the next. A competitive healthcare organization is near the peak of the infrastructure innovation curve and is exploring ways to make the "leap" to the final *S* curve. Other organizations have invested in creating the final *S* curve. Those creators are defining healthcare homes, accountable care organizations, and the model of healthcare reimbursement that will incentivize and reward improvement in health outcomes for the patient populations they serve.

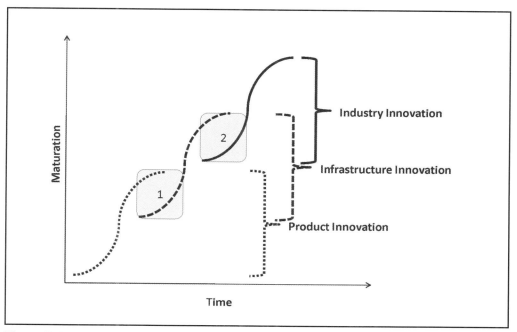

Figure 5-3: Innovation and Transformation

THE CHALLENGES

Transformation in an industry, be it healthcare or otherwise, is challenging on many levels. The infrastructure innovation layer of the maturation model has a great deal of dependency upon product standardization and a standardized delivery process. A typical IDN is not architected in a way that makes these transformations easy.

If we use Fairview Health Services as an example of a fairly typical IDN, we can describe several of the challenges. The expression "healthcare is local" suggests that the concepts of the service are fairly self-contained between the patient, physician, and services that do not extend far from this initial interaction. This is far from typical. Fairview provides care from more than 1,500 affiliated and employed physicians. That care is provided in more than 50 clinics and 7 hospitals that span a geographic area covering 350 miles, north to south. Those practices and hospitals represent the complexity of the academic medical center for the University of Minnesota, down to the community hospital located in Wyoming, Minnesota (population: 3,800). Standardization of products and services was not taken lightly.

The initial step in the process of transformation was to define a key group of constituents that could come together and both serve to represent the varied constituencies of the IDN and step back and understand the needs of the IDN as a whole. These individuals needed to come together to define a common vision that they could agree upon, sell back to the stakeholders they represented, and be able to understand that vision well enough to look across the industry and identify other organizations most like the organization that Fairview wanted to become. We defined as many different constituency groups as possible by geography, specialty, clinical and operational disciplines, diversity of background, and commitment to transformation. We then created a matrix of those constituencies against those individuals we felt were most up to delivering on the task-at-hand. We were able to develop a representative team of fewer than 20 individuals to accomplish this work. The size of the team was key on several accounts. The team needed to be small enough to effectively reach consensus on the identified decisions and diverse enough to be considered representative, but large enough to be able to accommodate overlapping viewpoints when individuals were unable to participate.

The first task of the group was to reorient their frame of reference for the work needed to be done. In a large IDN, it is not uncommon for individuals to become very "me"-centric. They become fixed on themselves, or their departments, disciplines, or hospitals. This is not unexpected because most of the support they have received to date has been a result of their own work or the decisions of their local support structure. We assist this transformation by identifying common organizational goals that all parties can rally around ahead of their own needs. We found that identifying patient-related safety, satisfaction, and quality goals were easy to rally around, especially when we would frame the patient as a member of their immediate family. Most of our team members had personal experiences with our or other IDNs and had plenty of suggestions for improvement. This energy and enthusiasm was leveraged to support the guiding principles as laid out in Figure 5-4.

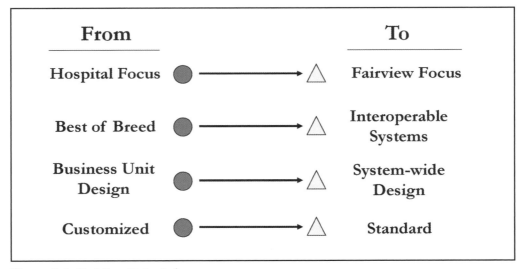

Figure 5-4: Guiding Principles

Each principle is really a variation on the theme of transitioning away from the ideology of an individual as the center of attention to a common set of standards as the new goal. Individuals realized the value of interoperable applications ahead of those that were highly specialized best-of-breed applications or those that had been so highly customized for their individual needs that changes would take months to apply. They also realized that the standardized developmental approach created an environment that was much easier to support. Systems that were easier to support would then be easier to maintain and update for ongoing organizational optimization.

The team members carried many of their own biases regarding technologies and were equally vocal about the concerns of their peers. Every one of the concerns was, in fact, valid. Opportunity arose to help team members understand that the challenges they were facing were, in fact, a byproduct of the decisions that were made and supported in their quest for such highly specialized and personalized application. Several examples are outlined here.

Redundant data entry processes were rampant at our organization. This was a result of the best-of-breed decision making that was done locally, with little understanding of the bigger organization or business workflows within other departments. Key workflows had entirely different vendor applications at either end of the process. In a few key workflows, this required staff to rekey data from one system to the next, the best solution despite the best organizational attempts to alleviate this process. In many cases, data could be moved from one application to the next, but typically in a "read only" format. Once available in the receiving system, it could be viewed, but little action could be taken on those data. We were good at integrating the information (moving from *a* to *b*), but we were unable to make the data interoperable (actionable at the receiving system). An example of our integration map is represented in Figure 5-5.

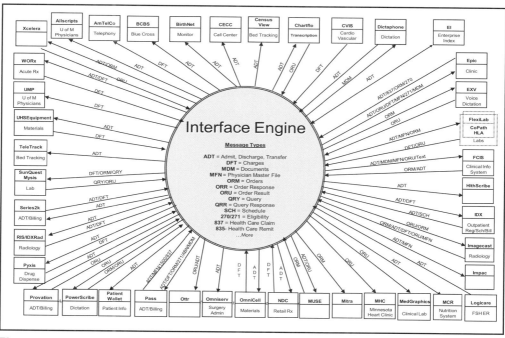

Figure 5-5: **Typical Integration Map**

Managing passwords was both a provider dis-satisfier, as well as a help desk management challenge. Our providers typically would have 5 to 10 applications they were utilizing to manage the totality of patient care. Despite organizational policy intended to simplify password management, there were limitations the applications themselves were unwilling to compromise on. One particular application required users to change their password every 60 days to an eight-character alpha numeric entry that had not been utilized in any of the last ten times. What at one time had seemed like a security advantage had turned into a user nightmare. Not only was this a challenge for users, but the number one help desk call for the last three years was password reset support. This was not a very efficient use of either the clinician or the support staff.

Application downtime and the associated manual workarounds had become the norm. In many cases, application users would do a majority of their work utilizing a personal paper-based system and then at key points during the day, they would transcribe their handwritten notes into the necessary computer systems. Staff had no ability to rely on the applications, as they could never be certain if the applications were going to be down unexpectedly. Worse yet were the times when the applications were not actually down but performing so slowly that they gave the impression of being down to the users. The absence of confidence in the systems left staff with little hope that change would necessarily equate improvement, so enthusiasm often waned.

One of the final challenges facing the staff was training issues. Fairview used a very traditional training methodology for technology. Users of technology systems were expected to go to class in advance of the system's implementation or during their orientation period. These classes were taught by either IT staff or staff dedicated to the process of training. In many cases, those individuals responsible for employee training knew very little about the workflow or processes these individuals were likely to encounter. Certainly, they did not understand the nuances of a similar process from one unit to the next. They failed to account for the fact that a discharge (transfer) from the intensive care unit (ICU) was a very different process than a discharge from the medical surgical unit or from the pediatric unit. The process was often complex enough that the real opportunity for learning would have been on the floor during the application utilization, but that was rarely given, except for a few 'at the shoulder' opportunities presented to physicians; but again, this service was provided by IT personnel unfamiliar with the nuances of clinical care.

THE APPROACH

The cross-disciplinary team quickly developed a camaraderie resulting from their common systems-level frustrations and the ease by which they were able to rally around the common goals that they could easily share around the patient and family experience. The team was given an opportunity to describe the current status quo and 'free think' a vision for a new healthcare delivery system.

It was natural for the team to begin to think of what they wanted to accomplish by going through and defining workflows and all of the features and functions that they would like to have within those workflows. After they were given several days to work their problems in this way, they realized they were in the process of developing hundreds of functionality points in each of the different medical disciplinary areas. They were, in essence, creating the evaluation element of a request for proposal (RFP). As many of the team members had considerable experience using a variety of EHR products in their current or past positions, they began to realize that the functional description and actions were going to lead them down a path that was going to be difficult to evaluate. They had a fairly thorough understanding of vendor capabilities and decided to abandon the approach of specific feature functions in favor of a process of defining and evaluating vendors on a process of core value satisfaction. Figure 5-6 demonstrates the core values that were identified and agreed upon by all of the team members.

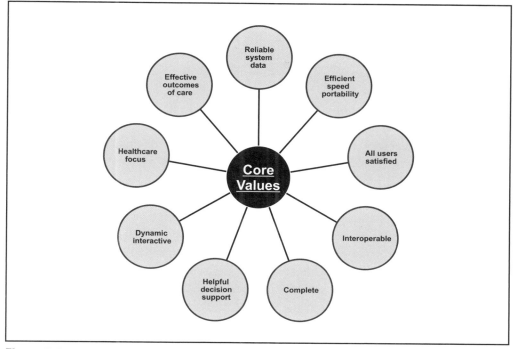

Figure 5-6: Electronic Health Record Core Values

The agreed upon core values and associated definitions are listed here:

- **Efficiency through speed and portability:** The chosen solution must enhance the efficiency of all those who use it by speeding up the workflows that are typically done, allowing for new, more efficient workflows and by providing tools that are highly portable, thus making documentation at the point of care a natural process.
- **All users are satisfied:** Anyone who is required to use the system must find use of the EHR to be a satisfying experience. Would the user be willing to go back to his or her prior processes of patient care?
- **Interoperable applications:** Regardless of whether the EHR solution comes from a single vendor or a conglomeration of vendors, data recorded in one region of the application must be able to move through the systems and be editable and actionable by the next provider utilizing the data.
- **Complete:** All the data necessary to render patient care is contained within the EHR solution.
- **Helpful decision support:** Tools exist within the EHR solution to facilitate caregivers' ability to effectively provide care for their patients. It is easy to do what is right and necessary, and it is difficult or impossible to take an action that could possibly cause patient harm.
- **Dynamic and interactive:** Data must be updated and available in a real-time manner, as well as be available for annotation, correction, and action.

- **Healthcare focus:** Information is presented in a way that facilitates the provision of care and is not just a repository and presentation of data.
- **Effective through outcomes of care:** The EHR provided knowledge to the user to facilitate achieving desired outcomes, be it through the delivery of evidence-based medicine, care plans, or best practice guidelines.
- **Reliable systems data:** Can you trust the EHR? Are the data there when they are supposed to be? Are they the right data that can be acted upon without question? Is the system available sufficiently to be depended upon as the ultimate tool for patient care?

In addition to the development of the core values to drive organizational decision making, the team identified transitions of care to be the most labor intensive and risk prone processes that staff and patients experience in the provision of care. A transition point can be described as any time the patient moves from one physical place within a healthcare system to the next. Typical transition points include clinic to emergency department, emergency department to floor, floor to surgery and back, and floor to nursing home. At each of these transitions, there is likely to be a complete turnover of the staff providing patient care, as well as often a transition from one record keeping system to the next. Knowing that the healthcare team cannot cross the transition, the team emphasized the necessity for patient care data to easily make this transition. In an environment in which the data easily transitions, the staff is relieved of the responsibility of having to entirely re-document the patient's history and course of care. This frees the staff to focus on education to the patients and communication among the care providers.

Following care transitions, the team highly emphasized the core value of clinical decision support and its support of evidence-based care. The ability to capture those elements of care necessary to feed the decision-support algorithms and then code the recommended action steps was a must. All members of the care team are overwhelmed with action steps that are necessary for compliance, regulatory, and quality purposes. Any opportunities for the EHR itself to capture, track and report on these defined pathways was felt to be a critical advantage that can assist in healthcare transformation.

Armed with a common vision and mission, agreed upon core values, and several targeted areas of absolute functional necessity, the team was ready to quickly evaluate a series of EHR options for the organization. To facilitate the decision-making process, members of the team decided that the focus of their evaluation should really concern only three options:

- Select and expand current EHR vendor A as the organizational core vendor.
- Select and expand current EHR vendor B as the organizational core vendor.
- Develop and enhance best-of-breed methodology or blended EHR.

Evaluations were done by doing site visits to locations picked by each of the current EHR vendors to demonstrate their model locations. We looked at two locations from each of the model sites, watching the provision of care and utilization of the systems. However, we gathered the majority of our evaluations through interview and commentary from system users at each location. Following each visit, the entire team would debrief and score the site based on consensus evaluations. Even after the final solution became apparent, the team spent a considerable amount of time analyzing their intended recommendation to be sure that there were no flaws in the decision making and that their choice offered the greatest opportunity for transforming their organization.

POTENTIAL SOLUTIONS

An abbreviated summary of the data collected is represented in Figure 5-7. Core values defined above were scored individually during site visits and then aggregated into categories of "ease of use," "user satisfaction," and "interoperability" to create a more understandable summary of the results seen. This simple five-point scale representation clearly demonstrates the predominance of one EHR solution over the others. It is important to note that all of the solutions had merit and a potential for success; however, Vendor A clearly demonstrated results that created an opportunity for transformation.

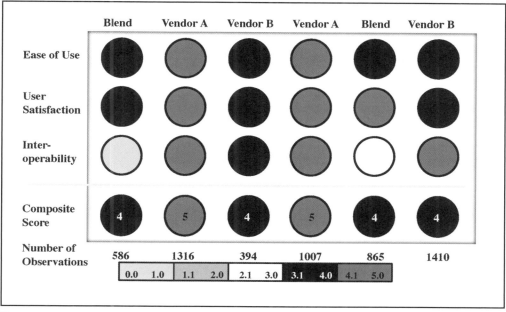

Figure 5-7: EHR Vendor Evaluation

The blended options whereby an overlay application would sit atop an organization's legacy applications had considerable merit in the evaluations but were not fully developed at the time of this evaluation. A blended overlay had an opportunity to leverage organizational investments in their best-of-breed selections but was not able to effectively leverage the data to be integrated into clinical decision-support tools or available as actionable elements for further provisions of care. This technology overlay is likely to be a viable future option for an IDN but was not judged to be sufficient to meet organizational needs within the next five years.

CONCLUSION

Medicine is a technology in and of itself. The CMIO has responsibilities to assist the organization in understanding and managing the capabilities that exist in utilizing medical technology to advance the causes of the business of healthcare—in addition to the actual patient care within the system.

As an industry, healthcare has advanced through the phases of product innovation and infrastructure innovation and is poised to make the transformation to industry innovation. The effective implementation and utilization of IT is imperative to this transformation. Careful guidance of both patients and providers will advance this effort as well. The CMIO is uniquely qualified and positioned to provide the necessary leadership to these individuals. Clinicians can be rallied around quality and efficiency imperatives to change their focus away from themselves and toward the patients. Patients can be rallied around the quality and financial benefits of preventive care and patient empowerment to become active participants in the healthcare model.

While not discussed here, the development of personal health records (PHRs) provides a technology tool directly within the control of patients. This tool can be used to assist in the transport of medical information between providers, as a recording device of patient-monitored medical data, and as a delivery mechanism for patient education. The evolution of the PHR as a technology in healthcare will be an important transformation to watch. The CMIO will have an important role in defining the interrelationship of these patient-owned records with those systems operating across the remainder of the healthcare continuum.

REFERENCES

1. http://www.merriam-webster.com/dictionary/technology. Accessed November 10, 2009.

2. Heifetz RA, Linsky M. *Leadership on the Line: Staying Alive through the Dangers of Leading.* Harvard Business School Press, 2002. P.13.

3. Kotter JP. Leading change: why transformation efforts fail. *Harv Bus Rev.* Mar-Apr, 1995;73(2):59-67.

4. Coffman B, Kaufman M. Innovation Labs. http://www.innovationtools.com/pdf/Innovation_and_Transformation.pdf. Accessed October 10, 2009.

5. Moy K, Ratliff G. The Aspen Institute.

CHAPTER 6

Nursing Informatics and IT-Enabling Technologies

By Donna B. DuLong, BSN, RN, and Judy Murphy, RN, FACMI, FHIMSS

INTRODUCTION

Nurses are the backbone of the U.S. healthcare workforce. Not only do nurses comprise the largest sector of the healthcare workforce, numbering nearly 3 million in 2008,[1] they are the frontline 24/7 caregivers to hospitalized patients. Nurses also comprise one of the largest operational costs to a healthcare facility, and maximizing the efficiency and effectiveness of nurses is essential to the integrity of hospital function and the promotion of safe patient care.[2] To maximize nursing's impact at the bedside, it is important to understand the role of the nurse, the current practice environment, and how nurses spend their time—all of which we will describe in this chapter. We will also discuss nursing workforce considerations and elaborate on nurses as knowledge workers. Lastly, we will talk about nursing informatics as a discipline and how, along with IT, it has an impact on nursing practice and helps mitigate the challenges in nursing adoption of IT.

THE NURSING PROCESS

Nurses have a systematic way of organizing and documenting their work, regardless of the practice environment, and this is referred to as the *nursing process*. The nursing process is essential to planning and providing individualized, patient-focused care. Five phases comprise the nursing process: assessment, nursing diagnosis, outcomes/planning, interventions, and evaluation. As illustrated in Figure 6-1, the nursing process is cyclical and, although the components follow a logical order, more than one component may be involved at any one time.

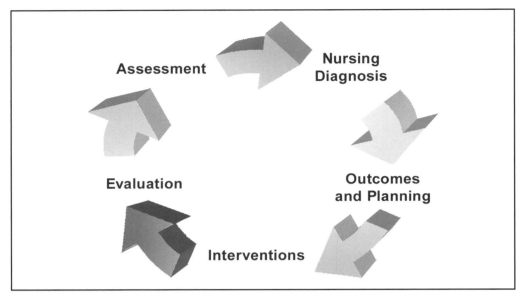

Figure 6-1: The Nursing Process

Assessment

Nurses use a systematic, dynamic way to gather, verify, and communicate data about a client, the first step in delivering nursing care. Assessment includes not only physiological data, but also psychological, socio-cultural, spiritual, economic, and lifestyle factors. The nurse collects these data by observation, interviewing the client and family, and completing a physical examination. This helps to establish the client's baseline health status, functional status, and risk for additional injury.

Diagnosis

The nursing diagnosis is the nurse's clinical judgment about the client's response to actual or potential health conditions or needs. Note that this is not the same as the medical diagnosis made by the physician. The nursing diagnosis relates to the *client's response to his or her health condition*. The diagnosis is the basis for establishing patient-centered outcomes and the nursing plan of care.

Outcomes/Planning

Based on the assessment and diagnosis, the nurse formulates measurable and realistic client-focused goals. This planning process helps to prioritize the activities for the client, and goals should identify the desired outcome. An acronym nurses use when establishing goals is 'SMART'—Specific, Measurable, Attainable, Realistic, and include a Timeframe. In addition, goal-setting involves the client and family, as well as other members of the healthcare team, to achieve the client's optimal level of health.

Interventions

Interventions are the specific actions a nurse must perform to prevent complications; provide comfort; and promote, maintain, and restore health. Interventions are designed to help achieve outcomes identified on a plan of care, and care is documented in the client's legal record. This assures continuity of care for the client across healthcare providers during hospitalization and in preparation for discharge needs.

Evaluation

Both the client's status and the effectiveness of the nursing care must be continuously evaluated and the care plan modified as needed. The evaluation determines how well the interventions worked, and the nurse provides a judgment about whether the desired outcome has been achieved; for example, whether the client's health is improving, is the same, or is deteriorating. It is critical to monitor and document the client's response to the care delivered, as well as to make continual adjustments to the actions taken to reach the desired health outcome for the client.

ROLE OF THE NURSE

Even though nurses are at the center of care delivery, on average, nurses only spend approximately 43% of their time on direct patient care (see Figure 6-2). What happens to the rest of their time? It is spent on workflow and communication issues, paperwork, staffing issues, information management, and coordinating care. Nurses are constantly responding to requests for information and assistance from patients, family members, physicians, and other healthcare staff. For nurses, even a simple task of contacting another department (e.g., pharmacy or laboratory) to check on the status of an order takes an average of four to eight steps that consume nearly three minutes.[2] According to a time and motion study done at Kaiser Permanente,[2] nurses in hospitals spend only one fifth of their time on patient care. They cite the need to "hunt and gather" supplies, complete excessive paperwork, and use outdated systems for communicating with other members of the care team as obstacles impeding their ability to spend time with their patients. The nursing unit is not always designed for efficient workflow. It has been documented that nurses travel between one and five miles on an average 10-hour shift, with an average of three miles during a daytime shift.[3] In addition, cost containment policies that reduce the length of hospital stays have substantially increased nursing workloads because patients are sicker on average and cycle through hospitals more rapidly. As a result, hospitals report high levels of nurse burnout and staff turnover.

Nursing Workforce Considerations

An impending nursing shortage is threatening to worsen the inefficiencies of the current nursing workflow. A 20% shortage of nurses needed in the U.S. healthcare system has been projected by the year 2020, roughly equal to 500,000 nurses.[4] The U.S. Bureau of Labor Statistics has projected a shortage of more than one million new and replacement nurses needed by 2012, partly due to the projected healthcare demands of aging baby boomers.[4] The nursing workforce is a demand-and-supply system that cannot keep up with the growing demand without a dramatic increase in graduating new RNs—a much greater pace than ever before. Roughly 90,000 new RNs are added to the U.S. workforce each year from domestic nursing programs; and 15,000 RNs come into the United States from foreign countries.[5] These numbers have been relatively flat for the past decade. The American Hospital Association reports more than 126,000 current nursing vacancies, accounting for roughly 75% of all hospital vacancies.[6]

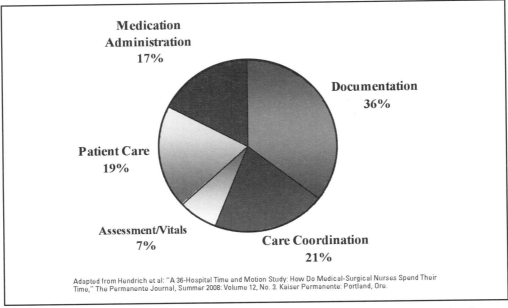

Adapted from Hendrich et al: "A 36-Hospital Time and Motion Study: How Do Medical-Surgical Nurses Spend Their Time," The Permanente Journal, Summer 2008: Volume 12, No. 3. Kaiser Permanente: Portland, Ore.

Figure 6-2: Hospital Time and Motion Study on How Nurses Spend their Time[2]

To meet this increased demand for nurses, enrollment in nursing programs will have to increase by 40% annually to replace retiring nurses.[7,8,9] This is very unlikely to occur, given that the shortage of nursing school faculty is restricting nursing program enrollments. The American Association of Colleges of Nursing (AACN) reported that U.S. nursing schools turned away nearly 100,000 qualified applicants in 2007 due to insufficient faculty, clinical practicum sites, and classroom space.[9] Nursing schools report more than 12% of faculty vacancies remain unfilled, with nearly 20% of faculty set to retire within the next 10 years.[7] Aging of the nursing workforce will require changes in the practice environment. The average age of the RN has steadily climbed to 47 years in 2007.[6] The RN population under 30 years dropped from 25% in 1980 to 9.1% in 2000, and more than 40% of RNs will be older than age 50 by 2010.[6]

The nursing shortage is real. Although some nurses may have postponed retirement due to current economic conditions, these nurses will soon leave the profession. One of the greatest drawbacks to a large portion of the workforce nearing retirement is the collective wisdom and nursing expertise that will depart without a chance to transfer their knowledge to the next generation because there are not enough nurses in the pipeline to take their place. The nursing shortage hits as longevity and more chronic conditions create a larger demand for healthcare and subsequently, a larger nursing workforce.

Nursing Staffing Considerations

Nurses are often categorized as one group despite different levels of educational preparation, licensure, and legal responsibilities. Registered nurses (RNs) are licensed personnel whose legal duties and responsibilities are regulated by the State Boards of

Nursing. Educational preparation for RNs can vary from an associate degree or diploma to a baccalaureate degree; however, there is rarely a distinction made in the practice setting for licensed RNs, and this group is categorically referred to as professional nurses. RNs must pass a licensure examination (called the National Council Licensure Examination or NCLEX) and obtain a nursing license in every state that they practice. Advanced Practice Nurses (APNs) with graduate level education can have additional responsibilities, such as the ability to prescribe medications and perform primary care duties as defined by state licensure regulations.

A licensed practical nurse (LPN) or licensed vocational nurse (LVN) is also a licensed nurse who passes an examination following a one-year curriculum that focuses on technical nursing skills. A LPN can deliver and plan nursing care but often does not have the legal ability to manage intravenous (IV) medications and often does not work in critical care settings like the ICU. Nurses' aides or patient care technicians are non-licensed personnel that provide technical assistance under the direction of a licensed nurse—such as an RN or LPN—and often perform patient care functions, including assisting with bathing, feeding, ambulating, transporting, or other activities of daily living. In general, nurses work as a team with defined roles and responsibilities based upon their level of educational preparation and licensure.

As healthcare costs increase, efforts to improve the efficiency of healthcare delivery must evaluate ways to improve the efficiency of nurses' workflow to ensure safer, more effective, timely, and patient-centered care. One recent study evaluated the economic value of professional nursing and how changes in staffing levels impacted the quality of patient care.[10] This study identified a correlation between higher staffing levels and their effect on lowering the incidence of complications related to hospitalizations, such as nosocomial infections, and their effect on decreasing hospital length of stay. Other studies have shown a similar relationship between a higher RN staffing mix and lower hospital complication rates.[11,12,13]

In an effort to improve patient safety, some states have introduced mandatory staffing ratios for RNs-to-patients in specific care settings.[11] While adjusting staffing mixes of RNs can have an impact in improving the quality of patient care delivered, it is not the only answer to addressing the escalating healthcare cost and impending workforce shortage issues.

Nurses as Knowledge Workers

Healthcare is an information-intensive business. Drucker coined the term "knowledge worker" to reflect the set of skills needed to work in an informational age.[14] Knowledge workers such as nurses work in rapidly evolving scientific and technical fields. Nurses are at the center of care coordination and patient management and must have the tools that enable critical thinking, analysis, problem solving, and evaluation, as well as provide access to evidence-based resources. Access to accurate and timely information is critical to the ability to improve communication handoffs among healthcare providers, currently one of the greatest risks to patient safety. Complex and dynamic healthcare information must be aggregated in order to be computable, allow personalized healthcare, provide decision support at the point of care and across populations, and enable ongoing research to improve healthcare outcomes.

It has been estimated that the scientific and professional literature in healthcare doubles every four years. Consider the demand this knowledge explosion places on healthcare professionals to remain current on best practices, quality improvement resources, clinical practice guidelines, standards of practice, and regulatory issues. In addition, consumers are much more educated about health issues; and access to the Internet, print materials, news, television, and social media have raised their knowledge and their demands and expectations for higher quality care. Nurses need to embrace advanced and emerging technologies as tools that help them access this information and apply new knowledge to practice at the point of care.

Sherman[15] acknowledges that knowledge is also embedded within the nursing staff, and one of the greatest risks to the profession is the loss of knowledge with the coming retirement of a large percentage of the nursing workforce. Knowledge acquisition occurs through continuous learning and the transfer of information from those who are highly experienced to those who are less qualified. As nursing expertise is one of the most valuable assets of a healthcare organization, it is imperative to implement knowledge transfer strategies that leverage technology and support the training and skills of nurses as knowledge workers.

Unfortunately, the complexity of nursing's knowledge base remains poorly articulated and inadequately represented in contemporary information systems. Today's systems tend to capture data for nursing tasks and have little basis in nursing knowledge. There is significant opportunity for capturing nursing data within clinical information systems, including data mining methods to assist with discovering important linkages between clinical data, nursing interventions, and patient outcomes.

NURSING USE OF INFORMATION TECHNOLOGY

Nursing has had a fairly long history of using electronic applications for documenting patient care in the acute care/hospital setting. Some of the early applications were available in the 1980s and focused primarily on ICU documentation of vital signs and hemodynamic monitoring values. Development of applications for the ambulatory and home care settings is much more recent. Even in the acute care setting, some of the more complex applications, such as care planning and bar-coded medication administration, have only been developed and become available over the last 10 years.

Applications for Nursing in the Electronic Health Record

Many of the applications for nursing's use in the EHR support the various steps in the nursing process. This starts with applications for the planning of patient care, or nurse care planning, including creating the problem list; determining nursing diagnoses; and planning patient outcomes/goals and interventions. Nursing applications for documenting the execution of patient care orders or completion of nursing interventions can take the form of structured or unstructured data entry and often use templates, forms, and flowsheets. This includes the documentation of assessments and interventions, such as vital signs, intake and output, patient teaching, discharge planning, and status of outcomes or goals.

More recently, application software for nursing has included the concept of a "closed loop" between the assessment, care planning, task list, documentation, and outcome evaluation components. This functionality actually parallels the nursing process and creates linkages between each of the steps in the process. With this functionality, the outcome evaluation results inform the assessment, which in turn, informs the revision of the care plan, and so on—thus, creating the closed loop.

Clinical Decision Support

There is often functionality in the EHR for support of nursing decision making in execution of the nursing process. This can take the form of synchronous and/or asynchronous prompts, alerts, and reminders during each of the nursing process steps, based upon evidence-based, best practice recommendations. The application can allow access to reference text describing the rationale for a recommendation or Web link access to online knowledge bases. Additionally, data from the EHR can populate concurrent reports and dashboards for monitoring and tracking nursing care and patient outcomes. Lastly, once data are collected in an electronic format, they can be analyzed and used for a multitude of purposes related to understanding patient care practices and concomitant patient outcomes. Data can inform retrospective analysis of the care provided and generate awareness of what nursing practices make a difference to patient outcomes, thus creating new knowledge and adding to the knowledge base for future evidence-based practice.

So, the use of computers in nursing really reflects a dual purpose: support of the concurrent one-on-one clinical patient encounter and the retrospective aggregation of information for analysis and generation of knowledge to understand practice and transform care over time. Thus, knowledge not only informs an individual patient encounter, it generates new knowledge for future encounters. Collection of this aggregate data enhances the evidence-based knowledge available in nursing and allows the learning of what care practices work and do not work in improving patient outcomes. Although some of this could have been done with paper records, the time to pull and analyze the data was prohibitive, as compared with the abilities of doing this using the computer. A whole new world is enabled once nursing data are coded and automated.

Patient Safety Support

A major EHR application used by nursing to support patient safety includes barcoding for positive patient identification and medication administration. These involve barcoded patient wristbands and barcoding on medications, in order to confirm the five R's of medication safety: right patient, right medication, right dose, right time, and right route. It may also include barcoding on nurses' IDs to document the name of the administering nurse automatically.

Other applications that support patient safety initiatives include order entry functionality to prevent adverse drug events, such as drug-drug interaction checking, dose range checking, and drug-allergy checking. Additionally, in the computerized system, significant events such as abnormal test results and duplicate orders can be highlighted.

Nursing Workflow Support

There are also applications in the EHR for supporting nursing workflow. These applications support nursing's execution of the nursing process and delivery of patient care, as well as help organize all the work to be done. For example, use of patient assignment software links nurses with their assigned patients in the computerized system, allowing them to receive notifications about their patients (available lab results, stat orders, etc.) when they log in. Automated task lists can provide a directory of "To Dos" for each patient or for multiple patients, during a defined time period, such as a nurse's scheduled shift. The computerized system can also remind the nurse of overdue tasks or contraindicated tasks. This helps nurses organize their work and ensure nothing is missed.

Hardware

When doing IT implementations, it is always helpful to remember the basic principle that *technology does not stand on its own*. It is used by *people* as they perform a *process*. Getting these three key elements aligned is absolutely essential to ensuring a new system works. Since the technology piece comprises both the hardware and software, the device used to execute the application is part of the equation that needs to be balanced. And it turns out that this is a very complex issue for nursing.

Some nurses are convinced that a fixed device at each bedside in patient rooms is the way to go. But others are quick to point out that this set-up requires frequent logging in and out. Others want handheld devices that can easily be carried into the patient rooms. But, this time, naysayers point out that the average nurse's age is now 48 years and that the small screens would not suit their vision requirements. They identify that not all functions would be able to be completed on handhelds, thus, still requiring the use of full PCs for some applications. They wonder about the connectivity and charging of the smaller devices and if two full sets of equipment (handheld *and* PC) for each nurse is an affordable and reasonable option. Other options nurses are evaluating include tablets, updated carts, and "med carts." The new tablet holds promise as a device that integrates the positive aspects of the PC and the handheld. But, not having a keyboard without putting it in the docking station can present some challenges with application software.

Most nurses today are using computers on a mobile cart. But here, again, there is no perfect answer. Some carts are lighter and easier to maneuver down the hallway. Others are sturdier and easier to move up and down vertically for varying heights. Some are easier to clean. Some have swappable batteries. Others have medication drawers, either filled by pharmacy daily or loaded by the nurse at the start of the shift for the assigned patients. This brings up the issue of medication location on the unit and how the medications get collected by the nurse along with the computer device, whatever that is. This brings up additional workflow considerations—more people, process, and technology interchange to consider in the work of the nurse.

IMPORTANCE OF INFORMATION TECHNOLOGY INTEGRATION WITH NURSING PRACTICE

Systems that support the professional practice of nursing are not just about the features and functions available in the software system. Integrating use of the software system into a complex clinical workflow is not easy—defining how the application will be used, on what kind of device, and how the nurse will interact with it requires detailed analysis and design. Adoption of clinical applications usually requires nurses to change existing workflow patterns and routines in order to accommodate the system. The process of finding a computer, logging on, selecting a patient, choosing a function and then completing the entry can be tedious. Consider the process for medication administration in an electronic system. The nurse needs to login to the electronic medication administration record (eMAR) or task list to see what medications to give—then find the medications (they may not be all in one place on the nursing unit)—then take the medications and a computer into the patient's room—then login to positively identify the patient and document the medication administration—then repeat the process for the next patient. You can see how the location of the computers and the medications will have an impact on this workflow and influence the efficacy of the process. You can also see how this process could affect system adoption and potentially encourage creation of a workaround if deemed cumbersome.

There are trade-offs (positive and negatives) with the different types of computers—fixed point-of-care devices, handhelds, mobile carts, or other remote devices. Often the nurse who "pays the price" by collecting the data and entering them into the computer may not be the one who "reaps the benefit" by accessing the data later on. All of these issues contribute to difficulty with adoption of technology during clinical application implementation, despite the fact that often these same nurses have embraced technology for numerous other processes in their lives.

Thus, it is important that nursing systems are integrated into the nurses' workflow and not "added on." Imagine the scenario. The computer system quickly and easily provides the patient's care plan in a way that highlights what needs to get done, what goals are targeted, and what needs to be documented. Appropriate decision support and reminders are available. Documentation is done at the point of care when care is provided, eliminating entry later and facilitating immediate availability of the information for other providers. All data are available at your fingertips. There is no hunting for computers, supplies, or medications. These are the kinds of workflow-driven systems that nurses need[16] (see Figure 6-3 for a graphic presentation of this model). The model also incorporates the concept that nurses use computer systems in the context of a complex workflow and also that they are the knowledge workers (described earlier in this chapter). In other words, nurses need to integrate the knowledge and the technology, within the context of a workflow, in order to provide optimal patient care. That said, unfortunately the vendor-provided systems of today are still more *data-driven* rather than *the knowledge and workflow-driven opportunities*, such as the one just described. Vendor product development is just beginning in this area, but it is where we need to go.

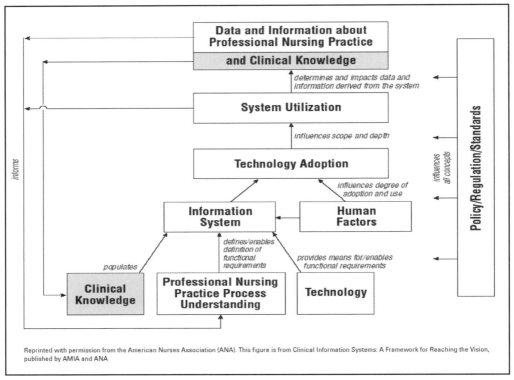

Figure 6-3: The Role of Knowledge in Care Process and Information Systems[17]

CLINICAL PROJECTS, NOT IT PROJECTS

In the implementation of EHRs and other information systems for nursing, the importance of planning and executing the project as a *practice* change *supported* by a technology implementation cannot be overemphasized. The IT components need to take a supportive role to the people/process/practice change being enabled by the technology. We need to ensure that IT is seen as the *means to an end* and not as the *end unto itself.*[18]

Four factors should be considered in order to drive clinical practice change and successful adoption by nursing when implementing IT. First, the project should be initiated by nursing as a professional practice change, recognizing that for technology adoption to become a reality, nursing may need to change its practice model, as well as all the corresponding job expectations, processes and workflows. Second, the project should be owned, sponsored, and championed by a dedicated nursing team that is empowered to create the future of healthcare using IT. Third, the nursing project team should be integrally involved in the design of the solution, as well as the training, go-live support, and post-implementation support. The IT part of the team should support them with detailed design specifications, system build, and testing, as well as provide input regarding the capabilities of the system's features and functions. Fourth, the training should be done by focusing first on the practice changes, then correlating how the practice changes were "hard-wired" into the information system, and lastly, how to navigate through the software application itself.

There is just no question that successful projects are owned and sponsored by the leaders and staff that will be making the practice change and will be benefited by the change, so only nursing can sponsor, champion, and create the practice transformation required for nursing system implementation. We are in the business of healthcare, and successful IT projects are not about the implementation of technology but are about the clinical changes and patient impact that is enabled, supported, and facilitated by the technology.

NURSING INFORMATICS

Nursing informatics (NI) is the term for the nursing specialty which integrates nursing science, computer and information science, and cognitive science to manage, communicate, and expand the data, information, knowledge, and wisdom of nursing practice. Nurses trained in NI support improved patient outcomes through their expertise in information processes, structures, and technologies, thus, helping nurses and other care providers to create and record the evidence of their practice. The definition adopted by the International Medical Informatics Association's Special Interest Group on Nursing Informatics in 2009 states: "Nursing informatics science and practice integrates nursing, its information and knowledge and their management, with information and communication technologies to promote the health of people, families and communities worldwide."[19]

In 1992, the American Nurses Association (ANA) officially established the role of the informatics nurse specialist, shortly after which they published their first version of *Nursing Informatics: Scope and Standards of Practice* and began offering the first credentialing exam. Although this recognition of NI is fairly new among the nursing specialty practices, skilled information management has always been a cornerstone of successful nursing practice. Nurses spend a significant portion of their time collecting and translating data for consumption by other providers, patients, and families. As computers increasingly become a tool for organizing healthcare information to make decisions, it is imperative that all nurses have computer competencies, just as they would with any other healthcare instrument.

Scope and Standards of Practice for NI

In January 2008, ANA published its fourth edition of the *Scope and Standards*,[20] including new, state-of-the-science material for the specialty and emphasizing NI competencies and functional areas. Overall, it articulates the essentials of NI, its accountabilities and activities for both NI specialists and generalists. Its standards are those by which all nurses practice NI and reflect and specify practice priorities and perspectives.

Certification for NI

The American Nursing Credentialing Center (ANCC) began administering an informatics nurse certification exam in 1995. The exam topics cover areas of basic IT, information and knowledge management, system development, human factors and NI models, theories, and professional practice. The ANCC Web site details the nursing candidate's qualifications for the informatics nurse certification exam, as well as the criteria for applying for the certification and the process for taking the exam.[21]

NI Roles

As nursing has been carving out an NI specialty over the last 10 to 15 years, many nurses have actually been informally practicing as informaticists since as early as the 1970s.[22] Many NI specialists unofficially adopted the role when they were selected to be the nurse member of a hospital information system project team. Often these nurses were the ones who had a knack for using the system on their unit, and, after the system was implemented, the nurse remained in the informatics role. IT departments, as well as nursing departments, learned the value of the involvement and project management skills provided by a clinically knowledgeable nurse. In their everyday clinical practice, nurses work with patients and families to coordinate multiple services and impact patient care. These skills translate well into implementing complex systems to patient care—nurses make great project managers.[23]

In acute care and long-term care facilities, as well as in industry or vendor organizations, nurse informaticists have held such diverse titles as NI specialist, clinical analyst, clinical project manager, and NI manager. Some of these roles report within the IT department; others report within the nursing department and have a close working relationship with the IT department and/or the education department. NI positions are also seen in practice as senior managers holding titles, such as clinical IT directors, chief information officers, and chief nursing information officers. The Nursing Informatics Working Group of the American Medical Informatics Association maintains a repository of NI job descriptions on its Web site.[24] The responsibilities can be varied and encompass workflow analysis, clinical system design/build, system selection, benefit realization and measurement, project management, health information system management, writing requests for proposals or returns on investments, developing educational programs, evaluating work process flows, writing policies, serving as nursing-IT liaisons, and many other responsibilities, depending on the role and organization.

The results of the HIMSS 2009 Informatics Nurse Impact Survey[25] suggest that informatics nurse professionals play a crucial role across a wide variety of IT areas. On a scale of one to seven, in which one is a low rating and seven is the highest rating, respondents reported an average score of 6.29 with regard to the value informatics nurses bring to the IT systems' implementation process. However, even the area with the lowest average rating (system selection - 5.12) still suggested that informatics nurses bring a high level of value to the IT arena. This research also tested the impact that informatics nurses have in several key areas throughout their organization. Three areas—workflow, user/clinician acceptance, and screen flow received an average score of six or higher.

Resources for More Information

The TIGER Initiative, an acronym for **T**echnology **I**nformatics **G**uiding **E**ducation **R**eform, was formed in 2004 to bring together nursing stakeholders to develop shared vision, strategies, and specific actions for improving nursing practice, education, and the delivery of patient care through the use of health IT. In 2006, the TIGER Initiative convened a summit of nursing stakeholders to develop, publish, and commit to carrying out the action steps defined within TIGER's action plan. The Summary Report entitled

Evidence and Informatics Transforming Nursing: 3-Year Action Steps toward a 10-Year Vision[26] is available on their Web site.

The TIGER Initiative was formed to help prepare the nursing workforce for the transformation to EHRs. In 2004, President George W. Bush mandated that all Americans use EHRs by the year 2014. As reported in *Building the Workforce for Health Information Transformation*,[27] "A work force capable of innovating, implementing, and using health communications and information technology (IT) will be critical to healthcare's success." Additional work has been done in developing the competencies of the future workforce as described in another publication, *Health Information Management and Informatics Core Competencies for Individuals Working With Electronic Health Records.*[28]

President Barack Obama continued this momentum when he took office in 2009, proposing to "Let us be the generation that reshapes healthcare to compete in the digital age." Less than 30 days after taking office, President Obama signed the American Recovery and Reinvestment Act of 2009, earmarking $19 billion to develop an electronic health IT infrastructure that will improve the efficiency and access of healthcare to all Americans. In addition to the substantial investment in capital, technology, and resources, the success of delivering an electronic healthcare platform will require an investment in people—to build an informatics-aware healthcare workforce.

This has accelerated the need to ensure that healthcare providers obtain the necessary competencies for working with electronic records, including basic computer skills, information literacy, and an understanding of informatics and information management capabilities. A comprehensive approach to education reform is necessary to reach the current workforce of nearly three million practicing nurses.

More than 100 nursing leaders representing more than 70 nursing organizations participated in the TIGER Summit in 2006 and developed a vision and action plan (see Figure 6-4). Each of the organizations participating in the TIGER Initiative agreed that nursing must integrate informatics technology into education and practice. Each has pledged to incorporate the TIGER vision and action steps into their organization's strategic plans. Each fulfilled a critical role by distributing the TIGER Summit Summary Report within their network to engage additional support for this agenda. A list of the participating organizations is available on the "Summit" page of the Web site.[29]

TIGER VISION

Allow informatics tools, principles, theories and practices to be used by nurses to make healthcare safer, effective, efficient, patient-centered, timely and equitable.

Interweave enabling technologies transparently into nursing practice and education, making information technology the stethoscope for the 21st century.

Figure 6-4: The T.I.G.E.R. Vision Statement

From the TIGER Summit in 2006 until now, these organizations, together with hundreds of additional volunteers and industry experts, have collaborated to complete the action steps necessary toward achieving the TIGER vision. Articles and presentations at regional, national, and international conferences have brought TIGER activities to nursing colleagues. The TIGER Initiative remains focused on raising awareness of the need to engage nurses in the national effort to prepare the healthcare workforce toward *effective* adoption of EHRs. This requires engaging more nurses in the development of a nationwide health information network (NHIN) infrastructure. In addition, nursing input is critical to accelerate adoption of smart, standards-based, interoperable technology that will make healthcare delivery safer, more efficient, timely, accessible, and patient-centered. More information on the TIGER-related activities and additional resources can be found at the TIGER Web site (www.tigersummit.com).[26]

REFERENCES

1. American Nurses Association. 2009. http://www.nursingworld.org/FunctionalMenuCategories/AboutANA.aspx. Accessed October 26, 2009.

2. Hendrich A, Chow M, Skierczynski B, Lu Z. A 36-hospital time and motion study: How do medical-surgical nurses spend their time? *The Permanente Journal.* 2008;12(3):25-34.

3. Turisco F, Rhoads J. Equipped for Efficiency: *Improving Nursing Care Through Technology.* California Healthcare Foundation. December 2008. http://www.chcf.org/topics/view.cfm?itemID=133816. Accessed October 26, 2009.

4. U.S. Department of Labor, Bureau of Labor Statistics. http://www.bls.gov/oco/ocos083.htm. Accessed October 26, 2009.

5. National Council of State Boards of Nursing. https://www.ncsbn.org/index.htm. Accessed October 26, 2009.

6. American Hospital Association. *Distribution of RN Workforce by Age Group.* http://www.aha.org/aha/trendwatch/chartbook/2009/chart5-10.pdf. Accessed October 26, 2009.

7. Hayes JM, Scott AS. Mentoring Partnerships as the Wave of the Future for New Graduates. *Nurs Edu Perspect.* 2007; 28(1):27-29.

8. Buerhaus P, Staiger DO, Auerbach DI. *The Future of the Nursing Workforce in the United States: Data, Trends and Implications.* Boston: Jones and Bartlett Publishers; 2008.

9. American Association of Colleges of Nursing. *Nursing Shortage Fact Sheet.* http://www.aacn.nche.edu/Media/FactSheets/NursingShortage.htm. Accessed October 26, 2009.

10. Dall T, Chen Y, Siefert R, Maddox P, Hogan P. The Economic Value of Professional Nursing. *Med Care.* 2009;47(1):97-104.

11. California Healthcare Foundation. *Assessing the Impact of California's Nurse Staffing Ratios on Hospitals and Patient Care.* 2009. http://www.chcf.org/documents/hospitals/AssessingCANurseStaffingRatios.pdf. Accessed October 26, 2009.

12. Needleman J, Buerhaus P, Stewart M. Nurse staffing in hospitals: Is there a business case for quality? *Health Aff.* 2006;25(1):204-211.

13. Cho SH, Ketefian S, Barkauskas VH, et al. The effects of nurse staffing on adverse events, morbidity, mortality, and medical costs. *Nurs Res.* 2003; 52(2):71-79.

14. Drucker P. *The Effective Executive.* New York: Harper Collins; 1966:1-5.

15. Sherman R. Lost Knowledge: Confronting the challenges of an aging nursing workforce. *Nurse Leader.* 2008;6(5):45-56.

16. Murphy J. Time flies—or does it? Why we need to move from data-driven systems to workflow-driven systems. *J Healthc Inf Manage.* 2008; 22(3):9-10.

17. Androwich I, Bickford C, Hunter K, Button P, Murphy J, Sensmeier J. *Clinical Information Systems: A Framework for Reaching the Vision.* Washington DC: American Nurses Publishing; 2003:53.

18. Murphy J. The best IT project is not an IT project. *J Healthc Inf Manage.* 2009; 23(1):6-8.

19. Special Interest Group on Nursing Informatics of the International Medical Informatics Association. Definition adopted 2009. http://www.imiani.org/index.php. Accessed October 24, 2009.

20. American Nurses Association. *Scope and Standards of Nursing Informatics Practice.* Washington, DC: American Nurses Publishing; 2008.

21. American Nurse Credentialing Center. Informatics Nurse Certification Exam. http://www.nursecredentialing.org/NurseSpecialties/Informatics.aspx. Accessed October 24, 2009.

22. Saba V. Nursing Informatics: Yesterday, today and tomorrow. *Int Nurs Rev.* 2001;48:177-187.

23. Murphy J, Gugerty B. Nurses in Project Management Roles. In Weaver C, Delaney C, Webber P, Carr R, eds. *Nursing and Informatics for the 21st Century: An International Look at the Trends, Cases, and the Future.* Chicago, IL: Health Information Management Systems Society (HIMSS). 2006:145-154.

24. American Medical Informatics Association, Nursing Informatics Working Group. *Nursing Informatics Role Descriptions.* https://www.amia.org/working-group/nursing-informatics. Accessed October 24, 2009.

25. Healthcare Information and Management Systems Society. *HIMSS 2009 Informatics Nurse Impact Survey.* http://www.himss.org/content/files/HIMSS2009InformaticsNurseImpactSurvey.pdf. Accessed October 24, 2009.

26. Technology and Informatics Guiding Education Reform. *Evidence and Informatics Transforming Nursing: 3-Year Action Steps toward a 10-Year Vision.* 2007. www.tigersummit.com. Accessed October 26, 2009.

27. AHIMA/FORE & AMIA. *Building the workforce.* 2006. http://www.ahima.org/emerging_issues/Workforce_web.pdf. Accessed October 26, 2009.

28. AHIMA & AMIA. *Joint Workforce Task Force report: Health Information Management and Informatics Core Competencies for Individuals Working with Electronic Health Records.* 2008. http://www.ahima.org/infocenter/whitepapers/workforce_2008.pdf#page%3D4. Accessed October 26, 2009.

29. http://www.tigersummit.com/Summit_Attendees.html. Accessed November 12, 2009.

CHAPTER 7

Lessons Learned from IT-Enabled Clinical Transformation

By Melinda Yates Costin and Marion J. Ball, EdD, FACMI, FCHIME, FHIMSS, FAAN

WHY IS CLINICAL TRANSFORMATION IMPORTANT?

To better understand clinical transformation, it is valuable to understand how this process relates to the implementation of clinical systems. Those who specialize in this activity are often called *health informaticists* or *informaticians*. Informatics is a fairly new science that ties the implementation of technology with the process of clinical care. It is often considered a social science, since it utilizes technology to enable enhancements in clinician practice. Reed Gardner of Intermountain Health Care in Salt Lake City indicated the significance of informatics when he said "the success of a project is 80% dependent on the development of social and political interaction skills and 20% or less on the implementation of the hardware technology!"[1] Michael Hammer, coauthor of Reengineering the Corporation, indicated "Change management is the hardest part of any of this...It dwarfs everything else."[2] Jim Markowsky, a frequent presenter on organizational dynamics has stated that "92% of implementations fail due to organizational change management issues.[3] The breakdown of why implementations fail has been documented as follows:[3]

- 42% Leadership
- 27% Organizational and cultural issues
- 23% People issues
- 4% Technology issues
- 4% Other

Based on these statistics, clinical implementations are now planned with a strong emphasis on change management. While it is possible to automate processes without change management, there is minimal process improvement and consequently the benefits are minimized. It is also possible to create enhanced processes independent of technology, but human behavior has shown that without an enabling technology to support the change, it is frequently unsustainable (see Figure 7-1).

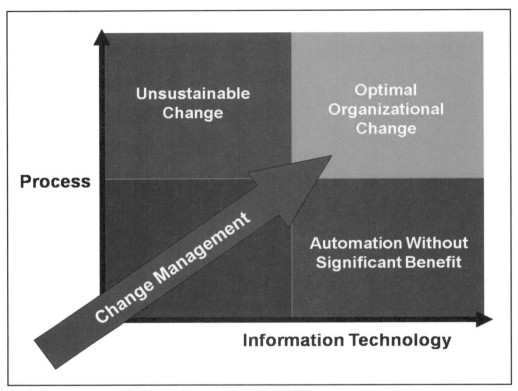

Figure 7-1: Change Management in Clinical Implementations

This combination of change management with clinical implementations is a huge challenge as organizations attempt to realize their vision. Experts in this field have indicated that "although healthcare is an information intensive industry and most people agree that information is power, it is natural to resist information technology because it changes roles in the social order."[4] Studies of companies undergoing major change initiatives, when asked what they would do differently, indicated that they would utilize an effective and planned change management program. The human factors related to clinical implementations are seen to be critical. In the Institute of Medicine's *To Err is Human*,[5] these factors are described as the interrelationship between humans, the tools they use, and the environment in which they live and work. Addressing these factors is the reason for doing clinical transformation.

WHAT IS CLINICAL TRANSFORMATION?

Clinical transformation broadly means assisting people in integrating clinical and non-clinical process improvements with enabling technologies. In Figure 7-2, the heart of the issue is the point at which people, process, and technology intersect.

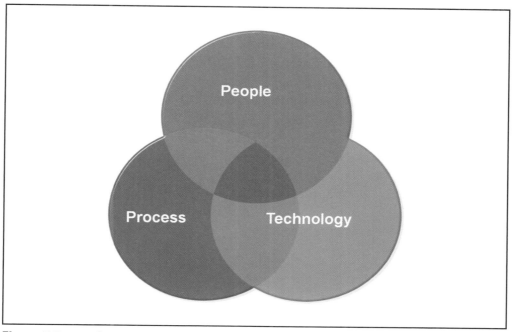

Figure 7-2: People, Process, and Technology Intersect

In most healthcare organizations, this activity is usually a system-wide collaborative effort involving all those who serve patients and is supported by an enterprise technology platform that:

- Creates a culture that fosters interdisciplinary collaboration.
- Eliminates unnecessary variability in the patient care experience.
- Develops and deploys best operational and clinical models proven to be successful.

In the healthcare industry today, the technology used in conjunction with clinical transformation is often referred to as the electronic health record (EHR). An EHR is generally not a single system but a collection of systems that address inpatient areas, ancillary departments, administrative functions, and the ambulatory environment. Considerations that are essential when implementing these systems with clinical transformation in mind include:

- Clinical evidence around best care.
- Clinical decision support tools (the ability to generate alerts and reminders for clinicians).
- Clinical analytics (the aggregate of clinical data that provides care measurement in relationship to industry goals).
- Governance structures that allow for organized and sanctioned decision making.
- User work groups that can provide input to process challenges, as well as areas for enhancements.
- Process-oriented education.

While the concept of clinical transformation has become well-accepted in the industry, it does change the entire process for how we deliver healthcare. The true benefit comes from behavior changes and, as we all know, change is difficult—herein lies the rub.

HOW TO MAKE CLINICAL TRANSFORMATION HAPPEN

Clinical transformation must be supported by a well-defined structure and enabling tools. Project governance is a prerequisite for any clinical transformation project. There must be an executive steering committee composed of clinicians representing the entire organization who are able to sanction enhanced processes that require a change in the current system. A typical subject area that requires governance at this level is order sets. Since order sets are interdisciplinary and are often physician-specific, establishing an enterprise-wide order set for a specific patient problem or procedure requires a great deal of collaboration to determine best practice. Gaining acceptance for a specific order set is more likely if it has been "blessed" and is encouraged by an executive steering committee.

Two additional types of teams that make up the governance structure for clinical transformation are the project steering team and subject matter work groups. The project steering team should meet regularly and address areas of the project that include project timeline, budget, staffing, and priorities. It is also the group that resolves issues, removes roadblocks, and provides motivation and encouragement to the subject matter work groups. Examples of work groups include an interdisciplinary team around operating room processes, including pre-op, intra-op, and post-op; and a work group around physician workflow that includes ordering, documentation, and chart completion.

The following are tools critical to the clinical transformation process:
- Key process decisions which frame the implementation. Examples include:
  o Will we utilize centralized scheduling?
  o Will computer-based practitioner order entry (CPOE) be mandated?
  o Will nursing documentation be done by exception or based on a full assessment?
- Current state assessments and future state definitions, which describe how processes work today and how ideal processes would work in the future.
- Scenarios which demonstrate how the future state will operate in "story" format.
- Process maps that demonstrate the handoff from one operational area to another.
- Test plans and education content designed around the future state scenarios.
- Revised policies and procedures that reflect the future state scenarios.

Figure 7-3 is a process map reflecting examples of activities that should be considered when embracing clinical transformation.

In Figure 7-3, the executive/physician leadership track represents those activities that would be executed by the executive/physician leadership bodies. Note that early in the process, these executives are crucial to the project in that they set the goals during an executive kickoff and participate in decision day activities that sanction the key process decisions referenced previously. Once they have a good understanding of the decisions required to achieve the future state and the time and budget it will entail, they then make the decision to proceed with the project. This is a critical step in a clinical transformation project, as this level of commitment will need continual re-enforcement as project challenges arise.

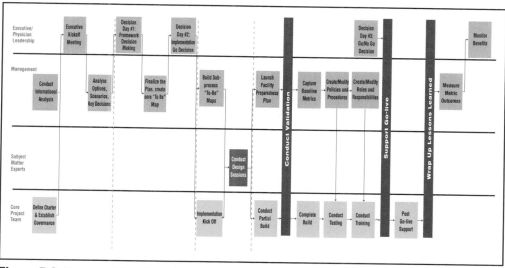

Figure 7-3: Process Map for Clinical Transformation

In Figure 7-3, the management track is absolutely critical to meeting clinical transformation goals. Without the involvement of key managers who direct processes throughout the healthcare organization, process change will not occur. It is this group that helps to identify current process issues and assists in establishing consistent and enhanced workflows for the future. They will participate in analyzing options and defining ideal scenarios. It is this group that will frame the key decisions that are referenced in the executive/physician leadership track. Note that it is also this management group that assists in the planning process for preparing the healthcare organization for their new world by describing what activities will stop, what activities will continue, and what new activities will begin. They also participate in defining base-line metrics, measuring metric outcomes, and modifying policies and procedures. Their operational knowledge and leadership is a major key to the success of clinical transformation.

In Figure 7-3, the subject matter experts track participates in the detail design sessions that are conducted by the work groups mentioned previously, while the core project team track represents the more typical activities that are required for any implementation.

It is important to also note in the figure that there are three vertical bars that represent crucial activities that cross all tracks. These activities are: validating that the system is being built according to the future state processes that have been defined, supporting the go-live activities, and reviewing lessons learned as the project is completed.

LESSONS LEARNED AROUND SUCCESSFUL CLINICAL TRANSFORMATION PROJECTS

Lesson 1: It is critical to involve the right people.

This includes those individuals who have awareness of the needs of the direct care providers and includes physician champions. Leadership personnel with strong project management skills and change management expertise are, of course, a core component. Another component that is often underestimated is the cast of super-users. These individuals should be identified very early in the project with a clear understanding of their responsibilities and the time commitment required. It is this group that will be trained first and will assist in the training of other users. They will also be the first responders for questions and issues as the clinical transformation process is being implemented. It is important to note that their responsibilities do not end after go-live. They should continue to be utilized as initiators and implementers of on-going enhancements. In this group, you will often find your best cheerleaders who will provide inspiration to others in the organization. Due to the large contribution that they are called upon to make, it is important to provide special recognition to this group throughout the process.

The patient safety and quality teams should not be overlooked as you embark upon any clinical transformation project. Not only are they often the first to identify processes that need improvement, they will also be the group that is interested in the resulting aggregate data, so they can measure improvements as the transformation project progresses. These people will be your greatest champions, as they see success and will also caution you regarding unintended consequences.

Lastly, round out your team with early adopters, late bloomers, and naysayers.

Lesson 2: Have a solid communication plan.

Provide communication around the "new world" your organization will be moving to and provide multiple methods of communications based on your different users, such as executives, physicians, nurses, and ancillary departments. Create a demonstration system for introducing the functionality and preparing people for the change in thoughtflow and workflow. Utilize a "day in the life" scenario, so clinicians can see how the new approach, using enabling technology, will enhance their environment and the outcomes for their patients.

Lesson 3: Determine and document all new key processes.

Do a short current state assessment to identify areas for improvement/transformation. Determine the future state and validate that it has total buy-in and commitment from the users through hands-on early review of the new workflows. Utilize a single tool to document all key decisions, who made them, when they were made, and why they were made. Create process maps for key processes and key department hand-offs and post large visual versions of these maps in the operational areas that are affected. This will not only build comprehension and enthusiasm but will also allow for critique and additional input from users in that area. Create a START, CONTINUE, STOP document which describes, in detail, those activities that will be new, will be the same, or will be ending for a given group of users.

Lesson 4: Involve the right people in testing.

Use real patient charts to create test scenarios. Significantly involve users and super-users in unit and integrated testing. Have active and continuing communication with downstream systems such as lab, radiology, and billing. Have users do unstructured testing, giving them the opportunity to try unique transaction flows. Test the printing of all reports and get sign-off from health information management and compliance for all content that reflects the legal medical record. Include medical devices early in the testing process, as this can be a very delicate technical challenge.

Lesson 5: Provide education around the new processes.

Keep the education team in constant communication with the project team, starting with the current state assessment. Plan on multiple training modalities, including e-Learning. Create a "practice" environment for early access to the system, so that users can sign-on, verify access to all needed functionality, and warn you early on of any issues with the new processes. Post the future state process maps in the training rooms. Plan on one-on-one training for the physicians, and provide cheat sheets and pocket guides as appropriate. Consider a simulation lab that gives users a more realistic environment for experiencing their new workflows. Plan for re-education on an as-needed basis.

Lesson 6: REALLY prepare for go-live!

Create a detailed activation plan that controls scope creep but allows for last minute required changes. Do shadow charting (have users work in their practice environment using a real patient chart) and consider double charting (while one user charts manually, another user charts in the system). In key areas, such as the emergency department and critical care, consider double staffing for the first few days. Plan for catch-up training and one-on-one support for physicians. Again, give plenty of attention and recognition to your super-users. Step up communications, including all-hands and departmental meetings. Conduct a go-live kickoff meeting with a topical or seasonal theme for all involved parties to generate awareness, enthusiasm, and leadership support for the go-live. Ask leadership to be very visible by rounding through all areas during the go-live. Follow up quickly on any identified issues, and prepare daily written updates and tip sheets. Conduct pre-scheduled conference calls that cover all shifts, so everyone is fully aware of issues and successes.

Lesson 7: Be prepared for post go-live.

Provide constant communication to the users, including daily posting of new tips and tricks. Allow for an optimization phase to follow activation within four to six weeks, and staff with sufficient application thought-leaders to truly create a positive experience. This results in increased acceptance, as well as more effective patient care. Acknowledge issues, investigate them, and create solutions using the same structured processes used throughout the project.

A final caveat: be constantly aware of Murphy's Law "What can go wrong, will go wrong." Have realistic expectations and always remember, "Be Prepared."

There is nothing more rewarding than successfully accomplishing a clinical transformation project. It creates an interdisciplinary team that is well-bonded and has the ability to continually enhance care processes and clinical outcomes throughout the organization.

REFERENCES

1. Gardner R. Davies Lecture. Proceedings of the Computer-based Patient Record Institute Conference. Washington, DC: CPRI; 1998.

2. Hammer M, Champy J. *Reengineering the Corporation: A Manifesto for Business Revolution*. New York: HarperCollins; 2003.

3. Markowsky, Jim. Organization Dynamics. Why Implementations Fail to Meet Objectives. Available at http://www.blcn.net/pdfs/BLCN%20Strategy%20to%20Implementation%20Roadmap%20 Presentation.pdf. Accessed February 8, 2010.

4. Stead W. Lorenzi, N. Health Informatics: Linking Investment to Value. *JAMIA* 1999;6:341-348.

5. Institute of Medicine. *To Err is Human, Building a Safety Health System*. Washington, DC: National Academy Press; 2000.

CHAPTER 8

How Are We Doing in the Health IT Industry? What's Working? What's Not?

By Kent L. Gale

INTRODUCTION

The information in this chapter is time-sensitive. Over time, the specifics decrease in value, while the generalities maintain their value for a longer period of time. My goal is to help the reader capture something of value before they finish reading this chapter. Challenge what is written here by asking what this means to you as you traverse this industry.

On July 20, 2006, *ABC News* interviewed Neil Brooks, MD, a family physician in Vernon, Conn. Dr. Brooks recalled a patient who was accidentally given a sleeping pill instead of the laxative he had prescribed. The mistake occurred because the drug names, Doxidan and Doriden, were similar. The patient continued to be constipated but was happy to get a restful night's sleep, he added.

While some mistakes do not have a bad outcome, others do. Most of you are familiar with the experience actor Dennis Quaid and his wife, Kimberly Buffington, had in 2007. Their newborn twins, Zoey Grace and Thomas Boone, received a huge dose of Heparin, which almost killed them. Though this incident was accidental, a study suggests that nearly 3% of patients in U.S. hospitals experience hospital errors that put their health at risk. My goal is not to beat up on hospitals or healthcare providers. We all work in them, or around them, and we know there is a great opportunity to improve. This chapter will refer to study data gathered through the research company KLAS Enterprises, LLC; the data illustrate how software and high technology vendors are improving healthcare delivery.

One of the things I value most in my relationships with people is transparency. You can trust clear communication, and you know what is going on even if the result is not what you want. In that vein, KLAS[1] tries to bring transparency to this industry by reporting the performance of hundreds of software and professional services vendors.

KLAS interviews more than 1,500 healthcare professionals in hospitals, clinics, and some smaller physician practices every month, completing about 27,000 vendor performance evaluations in 2008 (see Figure 8-1). This chapter discusses the value of our work in helping to create better transparency in the industry.

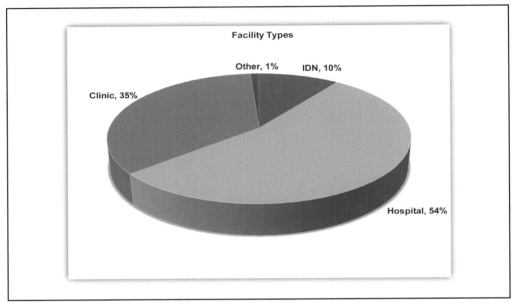

Figure 8-1: Distribution of KLAS Evaluations in 2008

Approximately 38 of us at KLAS speak with professionals at all management levels of healthcare delivery organizations. We spend less time with chief executive officers (CEOs) and chief operating officers (COO), who typically do not want to know much about what is going on with the software itself, and more time with chief financial officers (CFOs), who have a deep interest in billing, accounts receivable, and general accounting. During an interview, we ask the providers 40 questions, such as what software and/or medical equipment they use, how they like it, how well their vendor does its job, and if they are getting their money's worth. Much of the data is collected online, where providers can score the products they use. Because we have had a number of vendors try to score themselves online, virtually all online evaluations are followed up by phone calls to validate the sources of the evaluations. Vendor-scored evaluations never make it to the database.

LOOKING AT THE INDUSTRY THROUGH KLAS RESEARCH DATA

Not surprisingly, providers downloaded more reports from the Ambulatory EMR space than any other KLAS report in 2008 (see Figure 8-2). In fact, a considerable portion of federal stimulus money is going to go to this market space for physicians who have EHRs installed and demonstrate improved outcomes. Referring, again, to the figure, the market segment that is being looked at second most is practice management; if providers are looking to change their EHR, they will often look into changing their billing system, too. The next most-viewed area is the diagnostic picture archive and communication system (PACS) segment. PACS covers all kinds of image storage. We are now on the second generation of PACS solutions, so it is an area of interest to providers.

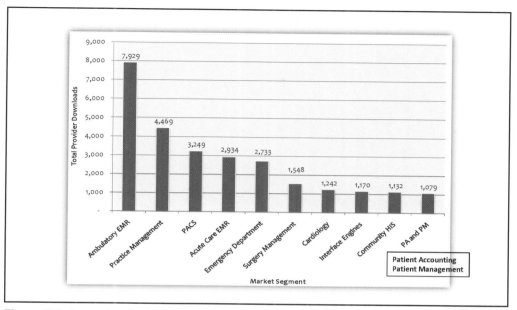

Figure 8-2: Downloaded KLAS Reports for 2008 by Market Segment

Figure 8-3 shows the overall average score of products in each market segment. These scores are good indicators of how complex and difficult implementing some of these software applications can be. Enterprise scheduling tends to be the easiest or at least the highest-scoring segment in terms of being delivered. It scores well, but do not be fooled. Enterprise scheduling is, to a large extent, ambulatory scheduling. Most organizations do not schedule much on the inpatient side yet, making enterprise scheduling more of an ambulatory solution. Enterprise scheduling contrasts widely with the acute care EHR segment, seen on the right end of the chart (listed as Acute Care EMR), and it is important to recognize the level of difficulty this segment presents.

Historically, there have been several approaches to covering all the areas needing software solutions. Combining *best-of-breed* solutions denotes picking the best products for the department users (independent of vendor) and then cobbling the solutions together to share data.

Sole source indicates a strong commitment to buy as much as possible from a single vendor, gaining from an integrated solution or one with transparent information-sharing. Right now, there is a real move away from best-of-breed to sole-source or integration. What is motivating this? Some provider organizations have 800 interfaces, resulting in pain and agony, which is seen all over users' faces. If you move to a sole-source or an integrated vendor, you tend to eliminate many of the interfaces. Take a look at an interoperability study from the early 2000s that is still relevant today. The sponsoring organizations wanted us to look at how well vendors were integrating solutions, and we found out a couple of interesting things (see Figure 8-4).

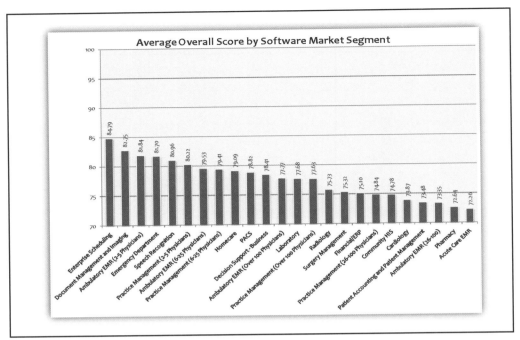

Figure 8-3: Overall Average Score of Products in Each Market Segment

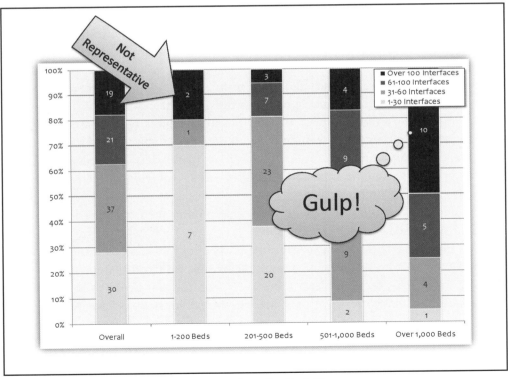

Figure 8-4: Number of Real Time Interfaces by Bed Size

First off, many hospitals we talked to with more than 1,000 beds had more than 100 real-time interfaces. This just tells you how challenging it is to have interoperability;

interfacing can be as difficult as communicating in a foreign language. For example, one provider remarked, "To call two systems *interoperable* means there is a free exchange of data without an intervening architecture other than a basic handshake."

Unfortunately, this does not exist in practicality. Some vendors commit to 'foreign' systems interfacing, using accepted standards (logical observation identifier names and codes or LOINC), wrapped in a standardized messaging format (Health Level Seven or HL-7) with some possible context sharing (Clinical Context Object Workgroup or CCOW). The terms *integration*, *interfacing* and *interoperability* are loosely interchanged by vendors and provider enterprises alike. This provider would love the free exchange of data provided by two interoperable systems. In reality, however, this only rarely exists. When you install a brand-new upgrade of a typical vendor system, for example, interfaces to some of the other systems suddenly stop working. It is not the vendor's fault—you wanted the upgrade, right? The problem is that certain kinds of updates wreak havoc with interfaces. A lot of the vendors have many gaps when it comes to covering all market segments and having their own products interoperate (see Figure 8-5).

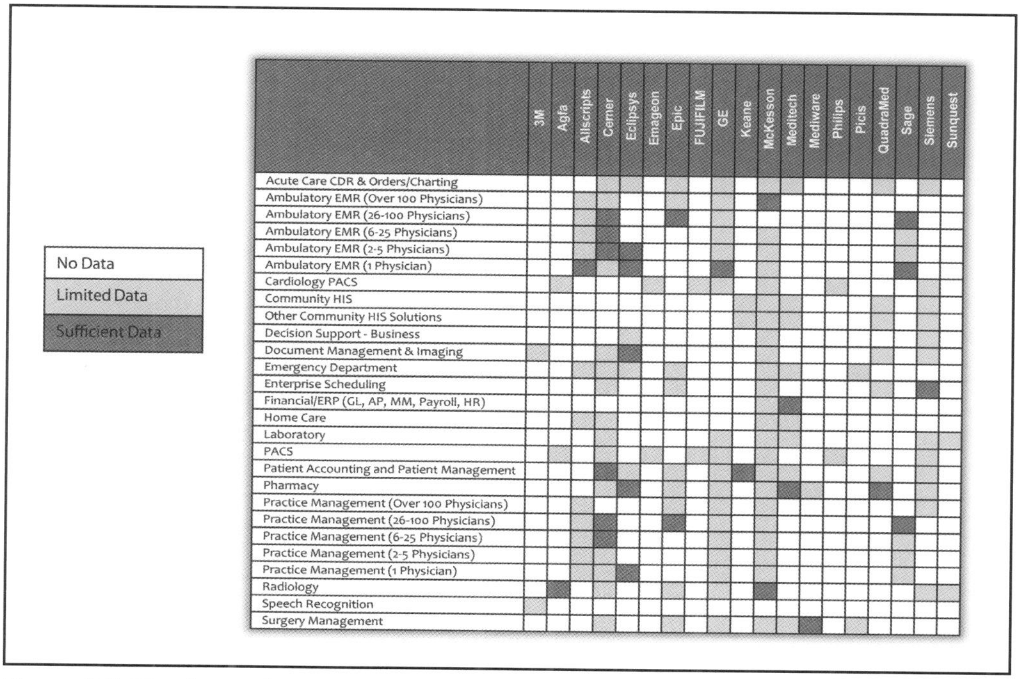

Legend: No Data / Limited Data / Sufficient Data

Columns: 3M, Agfa, Allscripts, Cerner, Eclipsys, Emageon, Epic, FUJIFILM, GE, Keane, McKesson, Meditech, Medisware, Philips, Picis, QuadraMed, Sage, Siemens, Sunquest

Rows:
- Acute Care CDR & Orders/Charting
- Ambulatory EMR (Over 100 Physicians)
- Ambulatory EMR (26-100 Physicians)
- Ambulatory EMR (6-25 Physicians)
- Ambulatory EMR (2-5 Physicians)
- Ambulatory EMR (1 Physician)
- Cardiology PACS
- Community HIS
- Other Community HIS Solutions
- Decision Support - Business
- Document Management & Imaging
- Emergency Department
- Enterprise Scheduling
- Financial/ERP (GL, AP, MM, Payroll, HR)
- Home Care
- Laboratory
- PACS
- Patient Accounting and Patient Management
- Pharmacy
- Practice Management (Over 100 Physicians)
- Practice Management (26-100 Physicians)
- Practice Management (6-25 Physicians)
- Practice Management (2-5 Physicians)
- Practice Management (1 Physician)
- Radiology
- Speech Recognition
- Surgery Management

Figure 8-5: Vendor and Systems Interoperability

There are a few things we do know. First, we know that no vendor has it all, and every provider has interfaces. By example, seeing that the McKesson column is all filled in, you might suppose there are no interfaces there. That is not accurate; there are many interfaces. McKesson has slated versions 10 and higher, which are supposed to eliminate many of these interfaces and, thereby, create a homogenous solution. In another example, if you are a Meditech client, you have many non-Meditech pieces that you still must connect. Meditech clients say Meditech does not like to have to connect to other applications. This is the real world. The second piece of information we know is that business decisions will dictate the provider approach. Standards help significantly, but required standards are still elusive. The goal in the next year or two is to get to a standard solution, so caregivers can push data around. Maybe this miracle will result from the American Recovery and Reinvestment Act of 2009 (ARRA).

Two years ago, we did a study that was sponsored by a customer who wanted to know if software quality is improving; therefore, we asked the vendors if they thought quality is improving in the software they deliver. Then we asked the same question of healthcare providers and contrasted the two sets of responses.

Figure 8-6 shows the vendors' self-evaluated scores from this Software Quality Study. The gap between the first dark grey column and the black line above it illustrates the difference in vendors' self-ratings between 2005 (the black dot) and 2007 (the dark grey column), a huge drop in two years. Why? By 2007, many systems had more physicians using their products to enter orders and to document care. Suddenly, the vendors recognized a gap here that did not exist before. More nurses and physicians need the systems up 24/7 and need to have quick access. For this study, vendors openly reported that they are not where they need to be in system availability.

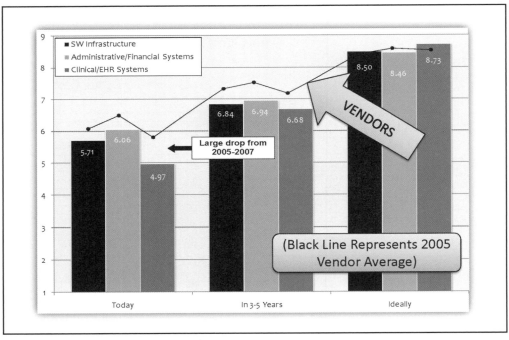

Figure 8-6: Software Quality Study

Figure 8-7 shows the providers' scores compared with the vendors' scores. The lower dark and light grey bars represent intolerable and tolerable severe issues, respectively. In almost every case, the vendors think their software is of a higher quality than the providers do. As illustrated by the "Testing Releases" column, the vendors think this issue is not much of a problem; for providers, however, it is a huge problem. If you happen to be from a vendor and if you have just entered this industry, these data tell you that there is a little bit of work to do. It would be better for the vendors to be more transparent and to understand what the providers really think of what vendors are delivering.

An additional issue of quality that the providers are challenged by is response time. Many older systems respond faster because they have been fine-tuned. Many times, the vendor will come out with a brand-new solution and nurses will be reluctant to switch. The first problem many nurses run into is that the software actually may work, but they cannot tell because the application is running slowly, with no indication of activity.

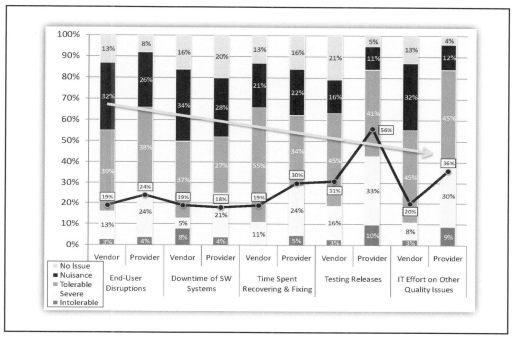

Figure 8-7: Software Quality Report

Vendor Performance in the Most Active Segments

Let us explore the area of greatest interest in the industry today: the ambulatory EMR space. In this space, physicians are trying to use electronic records in their offices, in which they are charting, e-prescribing, and documenting—trying to move everything electronic. Only a few vendors cover both small and large physician practices. Allscripts, GE, and NextGen tend to play in large and small physician practices, but most vendors play in one segment or the other.

Figure 8-8 shows how well each of the ambulatory EMR vendors (100+ physicians) perform in relation to their market share. The bottom-left quadrant contains vendors that have fewer customers and are not evaluated very highly in the survey. The top-right quadrant shows that the providers like the vendors that are working with the 100+ physician practices. Allscripts tends to be moving into this quadrant, and Epic is up in this range. So this chart gives you a sense of who plays in the 100+ physician space. There are not many.

There are a few other items to point out in the ambulatory space. Certification Commission for Health Information Technology (CCHIT) certification is important to some, but it may not be important to many of the others. Because there are about

100 products certified, certification does not differentiate the vendors clearly from each other. It is important to note that certification does not mean that the software actually does what it is supposed to do in deep use. Changes coming as a result of ARRA are going to open up opportunities for further certification pathways and even more potentially certified products to choose from.

Another important item is the structure of services models, with remote application hosting tagged as a win-win. Cerner customers were much happier after Cerner moved from PowerChart Office, which was hosted by the purchasing hospital, to PowerWorks, which Cerner hosts themselves. Why did this change satisfy more customers? The upgrades were easier to put in, and they were done by the vendor themselves. The physicians appear to have better success with the software services model.

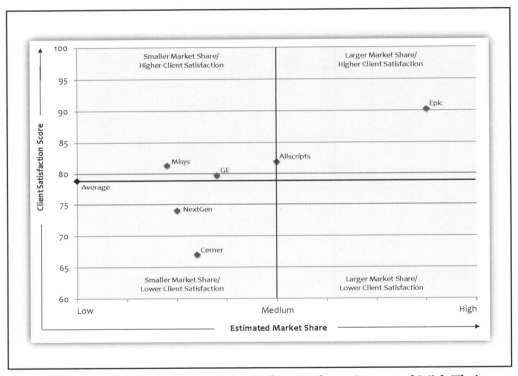

Figure 8-8: How Well Ambulatory EMR Vendors Perform Compared With Their Market Share in Practices With More Than 100 Providers

Figure 8-9 shows a list of the PACS vendors and how they compare over the last five years. The Community PACS vendors are those used in hospitals with fewer than 200 beds. These hospitals were some of the last to get PACS solutions because they did not have the funding, and it was a more elaborate product that they had to bring in. There are quite a few vendors that play in this space. This is a relatively new market, with many new players offering this software.

Virtually 100% of large acute care facilities have PACS. Now many of them are replacing the first PACS they bought with second-generation PACS, but improvements can still be made. One thing providers hate is downtime with their PACS. One of the vendors, Siemens, has been building a brand new PACS solution for the last few years, but one of the big challenges with any new solution has been that it was not found to be as stable as other legacy PACS products. That is one common reason why some systems get scored down.

Community PACS Vendor	2004 Overall Score	2005 Overall Score	2006 Overall Score	2007 Overall Score	2008 Overall Score
Agfa IMPAX	74.6*	83.2*	81.7	86.6	82.8
AMICAS Vision Series	**	85.9*	84.7	82.7	85.9
Aspyra AccessNET	**	**	84.9*	82.7	83.9
Avreo InterWORKS InterVIEW	**	**	90.9*	92.4*	93.7
BRIT Systems BRIT Roentgen Files	**	75.2*	89.6	82.2	84.1
Carestream PACS	**	83.1*	79.8*	83.9*	81.7
DR Systems Unity	81.9	88.6	89.7	91.1	87.3
eRAD PACS	**	**	53.8*	82.0*	77.9
FUJIFILM Synapse	85.0	83.1	87.0	85.0	86.4
GE Centricity IW (Dynamic Imaging)	**	95.8*	90.4*	89.0	87.8
Infinitt PACS	**	**	88.5	88.9	88.7
McKesson Horizon Medical Imaging	91.1*	91.5	90.9	86.2	83.2
Merge Healthcare Fusion PACS MX	84.2*	76.9	81.0	69.6	61.5
NovaRad NovaPACS	81.7	88.0	87.0	85.9	87.1
Philips iSite	82.4*	82.9	85.9	86.2	87.2
Sectra PACS	**	**	92.0*	89.9	90.6
Siemens syngo Imaging	**	**	68.6*	74.0*	68.2
Average Community PACS Vendor	80.8	83.4	84.5	84.6	83.2
Average HIT Vendor	77.5	78.2	79.6	80.4	79.7

* Limited Data
** Insufficient Data

Figure 8-9: Community PACS Vendors and How They Compare Over the Last Five Years

Serving Clinicians

Serving the clinicians is the fun part of our job. If Judy Murphy from Aurora Healthcare were to speak to this, she would say what the nurses say: "There is too much focus on computerized provider order entry and not enough on nursing" (note: quote from personal conversation). The vendors and physicians got very excited about the CPOE initiative, and they tended to plateau without finishing what the nurses had demanded a long time ago. The nurses went into a holding pattern in terms of getting new releases, while a lot of energy went toward getting physicians up and running. Figure 8-10 shows the difference for Cerner between estimated live nursing organizations and estimated live physicians using it. The gap is large for all of the vendors, except Eclipsys.

With hospitals doing CPOE, charting vitals, 'ins and outs,' and orders and results has very high utilization, as is seen in Figure 8-11. The tough parts for the nurses are care plans and ICU flowsheets, areas in which getting solutions to work well tends to be difficult. These data came primarily from chief nursing officers (CNOs), who typically brought in a nurse or an IT project manager who would speak to the real issues. These are the real issues they were talking about.

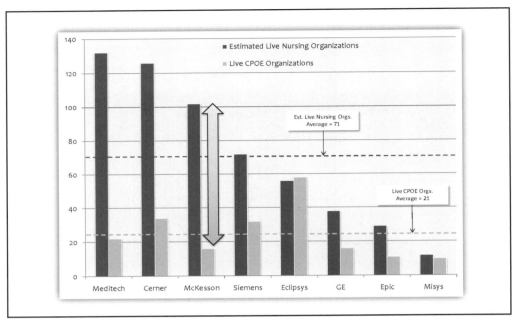

Figure 8-10: Estimated Number of Sites Live on Nursing Tools Compared to the Estimated Number of Sites Live on CPOE

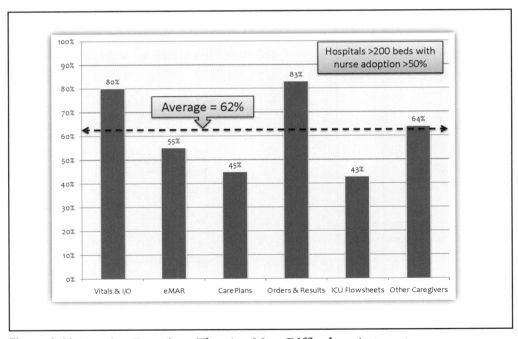

Figure 8-11: Nursing Functions That Are Most Difficult to Automate

Figure 8-12 shows what the CNOs are asking for: automated workflow and ease of use. The CNOs are saying that, with many systems, functionality is either not there or is really difficult to use. It is a challenge to use some of these systems, and that is where the emphasis tends to be right now. If you are a larger hospital, you are likely going to spend $30 million to put in a deeply functional clinical system.

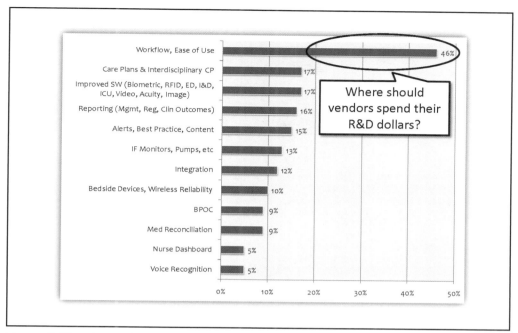

Figure 8-12: **What CNOs Are Asking For: Automated Workflow and Ease of Use**

There is a variance between the best-performing vendors and the worst-performing vendors. If the buyer is not careful, the hospital can end up with a product that does not perform well. The biggest gap in nursing satisfaction is in care plans (see Figure 8-13). Three of the six highest scores come from different vendors. In fact, a different vendor scored best on virtually every measured piece. Research enables independent application assessment and reporting. Other areas of large vendor variance are in connecting patient monitors electronically and in positive ID at the bedside for medication administration.

Figure 8-14 comes from KLAS's most recent CPOE report. This chart shows the vendor adoption in the number of hospitals doing CPOE. This chart can give a rough indication of what is going on with each of these vendors, but certain aspects of overall CPOE adoption can be meaningless if not looked at carefully across different measurements, such as percent of *all* orders being entered by physicians. We called a hospital to collect CPOE data and asked them what percent of their physicians were doing CPOE. Their answer was 100%. When we asked what percent of all of the orders were being put in by physicians, they answered 4%. The reason they gave was that physicians enter all diagnostic image orders, the only way they can put in those orders. As for the other 96% of the orders, which were medication orders—wherein lies the biggest possibility of error—these were not yet electronic. Based on that call, Figure 8-14 might or might not be meaningful. However, you can see that Cerner tends to be the vendor with the largest number of hospitals live on CPOE, which is good news. That alone tells you that people can actually go-live on CPOE.

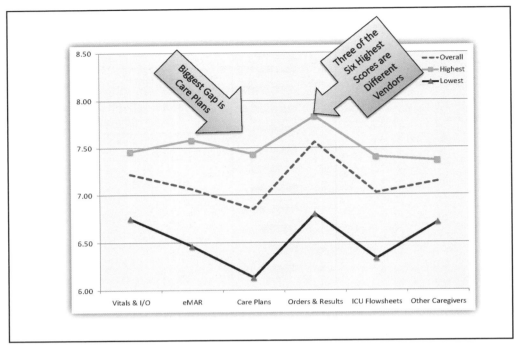

Figure 8-13: Nursing Satisfaction By System Function

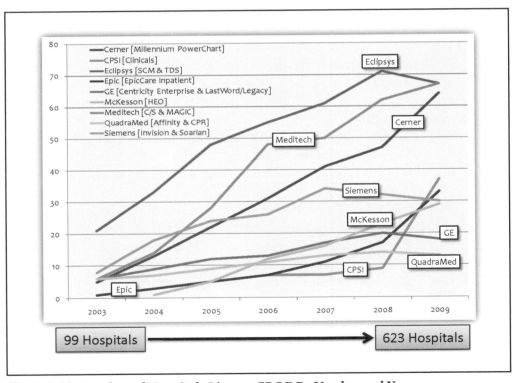

Figure 8-14: Number of Hospitals Live on CPOE By Vendor and Year

The bad news for CPOE is that there still are products for which the physician enters the medication electronically, after which the order gets printed out and faxed to the pharmacy. It is less common today, but it still happens. A few years ago, however, more than half of a vendor's sites reentered the medication orders. This was because there could have been a difference between what the physician ordered and what the pharmacy was going to deliver. For example, a physician may have said to administer X milligrams to the patient, which translated to one pill in the physician's mind. At the pharmacy, however, that medication was delivered in two pills. All of a sudden, the pharmacy had to discontinue the order and reenter it. Today, we have resolved that issue with most vendors, and Figure 8-15 shows how the vendors stack up in this area.

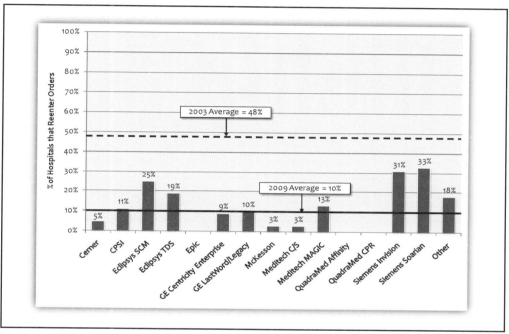

Figure 8-15: Order Reentry Rate By Pharmacists in Live CPOE Hospitals

Figure 8-16 shows the percent of vendors with their own client bases (200 beds and up) doing CPOE. The vendors whose clients have physicians adopting CPOE are represented by the higher dark grey column. This chart is very telling because it anticipates that a vendor with many clients using the clinical repository functionality for results review would likely have physicians doing CPOE.

If we compare Eclipsys to Meditech, we get a very interesting story. More than 50% of Eclipsys customers are live on CPOE, compared with 10% of Meditech clients (over 200 beds). If you take it to the next step with the depth of use (see Figure 8-17), Epic sites tend to have the highest use in everything, from bedside medication administration, physicians entering orders, and physicians entering their notes electronically. At this point, a hospital is getting close to a fully electronic record. Epic tends to have the highest overall clinical adoption per hospital. (This is the average per live site.)

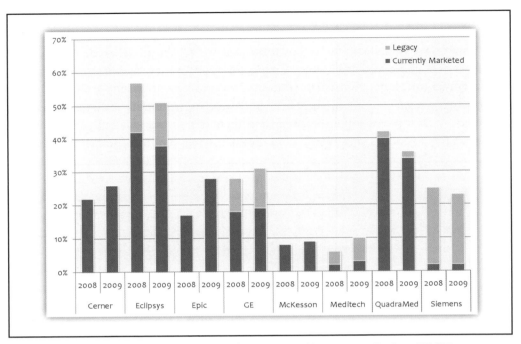

Figure 8-16: Percent of Vendors with Their Own Client Bases Doing CPOE

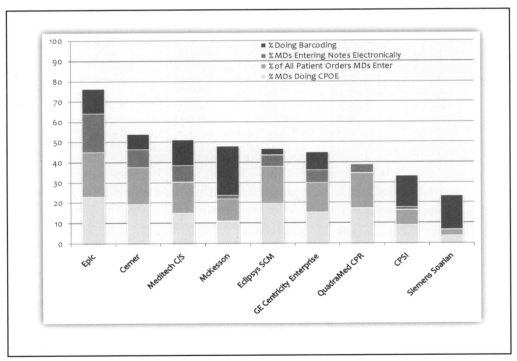

Figure 8-17: Depth of Additional Application Use at Typical Sites Using CPOE

The ED and OR are two hospital areas that are microcosms of all that needs to be automated. From these two areas, you have orders coming and going, results coming back, and charting going on. To give you a perspective, Figure 8-18 shows you how we measure the emergency department by vendor. You can see here the vendors on the left side and where they rank (first, second, third, etc.). Along the top of the graph are the different components of the emergency department solution and how well each vendor does them (based on a scale of 0-100%). For example, if we look at T-System, we can see that they hardly do any order entry or CPOE because the nurses, clerks, and physicians do not enter it. With Eclipsys, physician documenting and charting is almost zero on their ED system. EmpowER ranks third, and they have dark grey all the way across, along with Allscripts, who ranks second. This shows a deep use for those vendors in all of these areas.

Vendor (Rank)	Patient Triage & Tracking	Nurse Doc. & Charting	Physician Doc. & Charting	Clinical Decision Support	Order Entry (Clerk, Nurse, or Physician)	CPOE	Results Reporting	Patient Discharge
Allscripts (2nd)	100	100	91	77	95	95	95	100
Cerner (9th)	96	77	50	54	85	54	88	69
Eclipsys (11th)	94	38	19	44	81	69	100	31
EmpowER (3rd)	100	100	95	89	89	89	95	95
Epic (4th)	100	75	50	63	69	63	100	75
McKesson (10th)	100	67	71	38	71	58	96	79
MedHost (6th)	100	84	65	65	77	74	87	97
Meditech (8th)	100	73	20	53	87	33	93	60
Picis (7th)	100	85	82	67	70	67	94	94
T-System (5th)	65	69	100	58	8	8	77	88
Wellsoft (1st)	100	85	70	65	50	50	85	95

0-24%	25-49%
50-74%	75-100%

Figure 8-18: Measuring ED Solutions By Vendor

To summarize, both ED and surgery have great opportunities for clinician use. The challenging news is that the best-of-breed vendors tend to perform best in this space, which may mean the development of interfaces. When the integrated vendors like Cerner really develop this application, this will improve their marketability. Eclipsys' product is brand-new and trying to mature.

Organizations without a clinical information system or with one that is not doing the job might go out and buy a solution for physicians and nurses. Figure 8-19 shows the number of new purchases that occurred by year. Over the last few years, new clinical information system purchases have been tapering off due to market saturation in the over-200-bed segment. The assumption would be that once you have made that purchase, you are never going to do it again; however, that is not true. An example to consider is a system in San Diego. They installed one vendor's products. After two or three years, they decided it was not going to meet their long-term goals, so they replaced it with another vendor's product. That is an example of a multimillion-dollar investment replaced by an alternate multimillion-dollar investment, and this system is not the only organization that has done this.

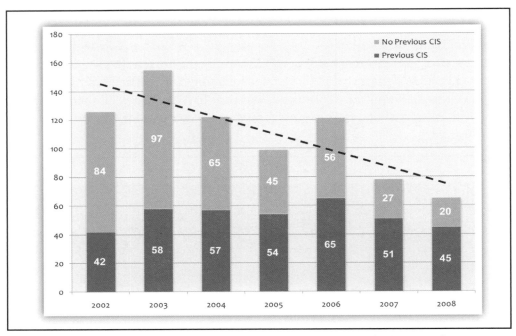

Figure 8-19: Number of New Clinical Information Systems Solution Purchases—By Year

Many hospitals want to receive ARRA stimulus money, but their success is based on their hospital getting to meaningful use of health IT. Based on the assumption that meaningful use will be defined as getting the physicians live with electronic use, Figure 8-20 shows that Eclipsys currently accomplishes this more successfully than any other vendor. They have 7% market share (the dark grey column), but they have 23% of all the physicians doing CPOE (the black column). Of all the physicians who do CPOE, 23% of them are on Eclipsys. If we look at Meditech and combine Client Server and MAGIC, they have 15% of the market share with MAGIC and roughly 7% with Client Server (total: 22%). With that much market share, you would think that a hospital would have a deep adoption and that the black column would go sky high. However, the actual percentage of physicians doing CPOE with these products is 3%. If a hospital has Meditech and hopes to get part of the stimulus money, they need to ensure an aggressive physician adoption model.

Finally, some organizations are talking about ripping out their legacy billing systems and putting in new ones. As some describe it, this process is like trying to replace one engine on a jet while the jet is flying, and then going on and replacing the other one. We went out and talked to all of the hospitals or organizations that have implemented a new billing system in the last couple of years, and there have not been many. The question to ask is "how many sites have gone live." If we look at the different vendors (Figure 8-21), McKesson came out with a brand-new product, HERM, (the dark square in the lower-right-hand corner of Figure 8-21), and they only have two pilot sites right now.

Cerner launched a product called ProFit in 1999, and when they installed it, some hospitals were unhappy with it. Some decided to de-install or not implement ProFit. Now, Cerner has some sites that are somewhat happy. When your accounts receivable goes through the roof, there are tough times. Cerner does a credible job in the clinical space, but the ProFit revenue management product is one area that is slowly maturing, as seen by the black line.

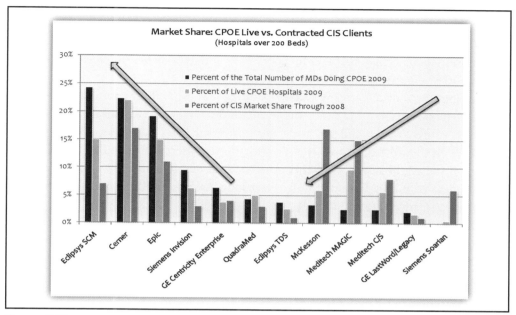

Figure 8-20: Success in Meaningful Use—Defined as Physicians Live with CPOE Use

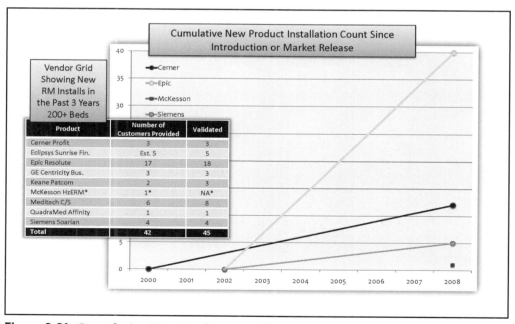

Figure 8-21: Cumulative New Product Installation Count Since Introduction or Market Release

Epic stepped into the marketplace a couple of years after Cerner ProFit and near the same time as Siemens Soarian. Epic Resolute inpatient revenue management did well with new clients going live. It is unclear exactly what Epic did differently from Cerner, McKesson, and Siemens, but they came in with a brand-new solution and had success.

At about the same time in this two-to-three-year time span, Siemens announced Soarian Financials and committed to having two hospitals live on April 1, 2002, after which they would bring hundreds live over the subsequent few years. At the time of that announcement, they had 800 Invision sites. Today, Soarian Financials is only live at about 10 organizations.

Getting a patient accounting system right is a lot harder than it looks, so we do not take casually the challenge faced by these companies. To a large extent, the systems that are out there are 20-years-old and have been customized and tweaked to the nth degree. The chart on Figure 8-21 shows the number of customers (provided by the vendors) that had installed the new AR systems prior to 2008, and it is not very many. We found 17 customers with Epic Resolute; it does not sound like many, but 17 customers might represent 30 or more hospitals.

Additionally, we found out that even the new systems do not replace all of the plug-in revenue management pieces. You still may have to use a third party (see Figure 8-22) for self-pay or third-party collection, as 92% of providers go to a third-party solution. In Figure 8-22, the black represents what revenue-management vendors provide in the software themselves, and the dark grey shows where providers have to fill in the gaps with a third-party product. In summary, legacy solutions with 20 to 30 years of heritage are common for billing. It is tough to replace something that has been out that long.

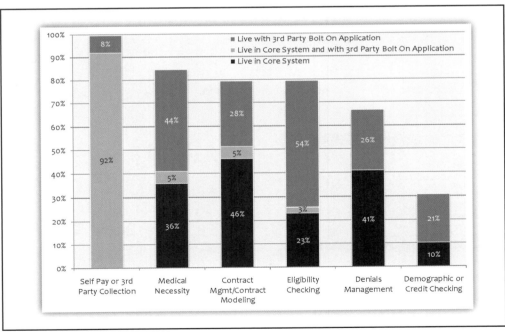

Figure 8-22: Revenue Management and the Need for Third Party Applications to Complete the Process. (2008 Data)

SUMMARY

Most provider organizations have a large number of software applications. It is becoming more common for a large hospital or IDN to have more than 150 software applications. When you see all the applications interfaced to each other on a chart, it is a mind-numbing maze.

When you factor in many of the new applications coming out, it becomes even more complex. There are applications for smart pumps and there are patient-facing applications, such as Microsoft's recently announced HealthVault. Connecting patients to their acute care and ambulatory records is very forward-thinking, but that is where we are headed in this environment. Google and Oracle are jumping into the fray. And to top it off, in 2008, Sam's Club announced they were going to sell the physician EMR, eClinicalWorks, from their stores. I think we are going to see more and more cellophane-wrapped software coming from Office-Depot-type stores. The real killer is going to be when the physician gets it, unwraps it, turns it on and tries to connect it to the unique venues in his geography, such as a local reference lab or other places with which they traditionally connect to get data. Odds are that the interoperability is not going to be there, and they will end up getting a faxed document to their office, and their clerk will key in the numbers. There is always a possibility for error in that.

You can just see that it is not as easy as it looks. At some point, we may all enjoy plug-and-play connectivity. For the time being, the performance really does vary greatly by vendor and product. Additionally, you can see that different vendors take the lead at different times, depending on when they release their products and the time that they have to develop and enhance the software. In the end, this is continuing to make all our lives more exciting.

REFERENCE

1. KLAS. http://www.klasresearch.com/Klas/Site/About/Company.aspx. Accessed November 20, 2009.

CHAPTER 9

Wrapping It Up: The CEO Perspective on Technologies in Healthcare

By T. Douglas Lawson

INTRODUCTION

With failure rates for new initiatives being quoted as high as 70%,[1] and EMR failure rates being widely cited as high as 50%, it is no wonder that a premium is placed on effective change management strategies. Central to an effective change management strategy is the composition of the leadership team and the related commitment of the organization's senior leaders to seeing any change initiatives through to completion.

BACKGROUND

Baylor Health Care System (BHCS) is one of the largest not-for-profit healthcare systems in the Dallas Fort Worth (DFW) metroplex and has been publicly recognized for its work in a number of key areas, including the advancement of IT as a tool to improve the quality care for patients.

Baylor Regional Medical Center at Grapevine (BRMCG) joined BHCS in 1981. Grapevine is licensed as a 249-bed not-for-profit acute care hospital with a total service area of 830,000 people and provides an array of comprehensive services. However, Grapevine is best known for Women's & Children Services, where more than 3,500 babies are delivered each year. We are also known for providing exceptional care in our Emergency Department (ED), in which we cared for more than 50,000 patients in fiscal year 2009. Grapevine is one of seven general acute care hospitals in the BHCS, and we rank third in inpatient admissions and second in net patient revenues. We serve as the system's regional anchor for one of the fastest growing areas in the DFW metroplex.

Our organization, not unlike many others, is under significant pressure to perform at higher and higher levels of quality, efficiency, and economic performance. As our surrounding communities have grown and evolved, so have their expectations of the local community hospital. As we have matured and developed our hospital, we have supported a number of very important change management initiatives that have created the synergy necessary to move forward with our EMR. The common themes of leadership and change management are central to this discussion and have been a critical success factor in our work over the past two years.

LEADERSHIP IS KEY

In any hospital, particularly ours, the organizational structure is a key enabler in achieving the vision. Our structure begins and ends with our patients and families. We place our patients and families at the top of our organizational chart, not only symbolically to recognize that our reason for being is to serve those patients and families, but to also understand that the priorities on any given day revolve around these same individuals.

The primary role of any leader is to ensure that an effective leadership team is in place, and this is especially critical as we grow and develop our hospital in a manner that brings value to our surrounding communities. Our hospital is defined by our leadership team and our ability as leaders to set an expectation of excellence as a critical factor. As leaders, we are called upon to set the example, to 'walk the talk' and also to ensure that our teams have the resources necessary to successfully achieve the goals that we have set. However, my four-year-old son puts it in simpler terms: "Daddy, you are like Sir Topham Hat from the Island of Sodor." I assume he means that my job is to avoid delay and confusion.

I put it another way. I would say my real job is knowing when to start fires, creating the burning platform for people to move forward, and knowing when and how to put the fires out. Developing leadership as a foundational priority occurs at multiple levels. As we move through the next significant evolution of our healthcare systems, our success will also be tied to our ability to identify and develop our physician leaders. The key to that development is the identification of formal and informal physician leaders who will help drive new initiatives throughout the organization.

ALIGNMENT OF GOALS

The way we approach the work within BHCS is truly based upon our vision: "To be trusted as the best place to give and receive safe, quality and compassionate care;" our mission: "Founded as a Christian ministry of healing, BHCS exists to serve all people through exemplary healthcare, education, reserves and community service;" and through our focus on four key areas: "People, Quality, Service, and Finance." Our focus on those four core areas positions us to break down the vision of the organization in a manner easily communicated to our staff and to our communities. It allows us to allocate our resources in a much more logical fashion and begins the hard work of aligning the work that occurs at the bedside with the overall direction of the organization.

Key to achieving our vision is the hard work of aligning the activities occurring at every patient's bedside with the organization's overall goals and objectives. This alignment puts us in the best position to maximize limited resources in a manner that optimizes care at the bedside and brings value to our patients, families, physicians, and the communities that we serve. In a perfect world, we would see a nurse assigned to every patient and an abundance of support staff. Unfortunately, we do not live in that world, and on any given day, it is the responsibility of our leadership team to allocate those scarce resources in a manner that promotes a safe, quality, and healing environment.

Our Circle of Care works in tandem with BHCS's values of Integrity, Servanthood, Quality, Innovation, and Stewardship. These five values work to define our approach in selecting individuals to join our teams. In essence, our values work together with our Circle of Care to create the alignment of our board of trustees, our patients and families, our staff, and our physicians. Our values are central to achieving our vision of being trusted as the best place to give and receive safe, quality, and compassionate care (see Figure 9-1).

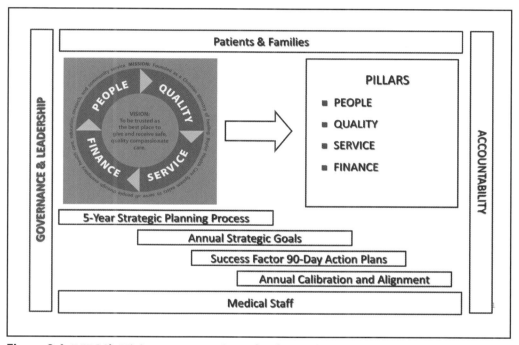

Figure 9-1: BHCS's Vision – Integration of Values, Alignment, and the Circle of Care

I spend quite a bit of time talking about this process to individuals joining our team, and I always end with a discussion of accountability. We are a high accountability organization. Our work is important work, and we take that work very seriously. We have fun doing it, and this is a great place to work. However, we hold ourselves and our teams accountable to a higher standard than most, and the pursuit of excellence in all areas is a core expectation. Those individuals interested in joining a high-performing team and being a part of a very special organization get very excited about joining BHCS.

Our commitment to excellence in each of our four pillars is directly connected to our ability to harvest data in a consistent manner and then, in turn, benchmark the results of our work in each of these areas against our sister hospitals across BHCS, as well as the best hospitals and health systems across the state and nation. With our goal of delivering best-in-class outcomes in each of the four pillars, comes a strategic imperative to view IT as a key enabler of our organization. This, in turn, impacts our analysis of IT expenditures and sets the backdrop for our support of IT projects.

STRATEGIC PLANNING: THE BALDRIGE PLANNING FRAMEWORK

Much of the work we discussed is centered on the use of the Baldrige planning model.[2] The primary reason that our leadership team chose the Baldrige Model was because it gives us the tools to focus on overall organizational excellence. It also aligns our Circle of Care with the day-to-day work that occurs throughout the hospital. It connects the thousands of daily acts of 1,200 people with our vision to be trusted as the best place to give and receive safe, quality, compassionate care.

We did not adopt this model with the intention of winning an award but to use this methodology to align and amplify our existing efforts to improve our overall organizational performance. This process is helping us transform our hospital (to paraphrase Jim Collins) "From Good to Great."[3]

Process in Action

When I arrived at Grapevine almost two years ago, the team was in the midst of dealing with a major challenge in our ED. Our ED had been ranked in the bottom 10% of hospitals nationally in patient satisfaction, with an average wait time of almost four hours, and with 6.3% of our patients leaving without being seen. We were clearly not meeting our patients' expectations. Not surprisingly, many in our community were traveling outside our service area for medical emergencies. You might ask (as our board did) what we were doing about this. We were very fortunate in that we had an outstanding team of clinical and administrative leaders committed to studying and learning from some of the best EDs in the country, and more importantly, to implementing those best practices at Grapevine. The results have been nothing short of dramatic.

Approximately one year later, our team had reduced the total length of stay in our ED by 32% and transformed the ED from being in the bottom 10% for overall patient satisfaction to being in the top 10%. Additionally, we decreased the percentage of patients leaving without being seen to less than 1.5%. That means more than 1,800 patients seen in FY2009 would not have been treated in our facilities without these improvements. As a direct result, our ED volumes have increased more than 23%, and we have sustained this level of excellence over the past two years.

The results we have achieved in our ED have created the momentum for changes across the hospital. As a result, we have seen improvements in almost every area of the organization, including improvements in staff satisfaction and retention and enhanced quality metrics, improved patient satisfaction, and organizational growth.

Success breeds success. You could see our confidence grow as goals were achieved and new improvements initiated. The most exciting part to watch, and one of our most difficult challenges, is sustaining this high level of performance.

Without question, our ability to translate and align the work we are doing to be the preferred workplace, improve our quality outcomes, and enhance our patient satisfaction is resulting in organizational growth. This focus on overall organizational excellence has given us an important competitive advantage in a very competitive market. But, the patients are the real beneficiaries.

One of the most difficult challenges we face as leaders is the work in taking a team that is doing good work and inspiring that team to do great work. I truly believe that is one of the most difficult challenges we face in healthcare. While we have a number of hospitals committed to doing good work, we do not have enough organizations committed to doing *excellent* work. My experience with the Baldrige Model has led me to believe that the use of their healthcare criteria for excellence and their framework puts us in the best position to truly achieve and sustain excellence.

I am truly convinced that central to this discussion is the concept of an information-driven organization. Where data are important, trended data are essential. Our ability to trend clinical information and outcome data and reduce variation is the only way we will see exponential improvements in the quality of care for our patients. This is critically important as we move forward with the development and implementation of EMRs. These installations represent important advances for many of our nation's hospitals. However, they also represent extreme changes in many of our daily processes, and therefore, notably, the law of unintended consequences is also in play.

Work in Progress

I really see my role in the installation of complicated information systems as one of ensuring that our leaders have a shared understanding of the organizational impact these changes have at multiple levels throughout our hospital. Aligned with this understanding, we must also ensure that our clinical leaders have related tools to manage this very difficult, and often emotional, change process. We no longer have computer systems that merely drive our back offices or serve as analytic tools. Our computer systems are now front and center in the patient care process. This means we must treat our information systems with the same care that we use for our MRIs, CT scanners, and other diagnostic tools. As we go about the processes of installing these systems, changes are forcing the discussion of best practice and the strategic implications are significant.

As John P. Kotter said in "Leading Change:"[4]

"Without much experience, we often don't adequately appreciate a crucial fact: that changing highly interdependent settings is extremely difficult because, ultimately, you have to change nearly everything. Because of all the interconnections, you can really move just one element by itself. You have to move dozens or hundreds or thousands of elements, which is difficult and time-consuming and can rarely if ever be accomplished by just a few people."

I finish with this quote because I truly believe the key element to the successful implementation of an EMR is leadership. Our ability as leaders to combine the appropriate team of individuals to be involved in the development and implementation of these extremely complicated systems is absolutely critical, and our ability and willingness to commit required human resources to the pursuit of this process will be key.

REFERENCES

1. Cracking the code of change. *Harv Bus Rev.* 2000;78(3):133-141, 216.

2. http://www.baldrige.nist.gov/. Accessed November 12, 2009.

3. Collins, Jim: Good to Great: why some companies make the leap…and others don't. Haper Collins, New York. 2001.

4. Leading change: Why transformation efforts fail. *Harv Bus Rev.* 1995;73(2):59-67.

Acronyms Used in this Book

AACN	American Association of Colleges of Nursing
AAN	American Academy of Nursing
AHIMA/FORE	American Health Information Management Systems Foundation of Record Education
AHIP	America's Health Insurance Plans
AHRQ	Agency for Healthcare Research and Quality
AMIA	American Medical Informatics Association
ANCC	American Nursing Credentialing Center
APN	advanced practice nurse
ARRA	American Recovery and Reinvestment Act of 2009
ATA	American Telemedicine Association
BHCS	Baylor Health Care System
BRMCG	Baylor Regional Medical Center at Grapevine
CBO	Congressional Budget Office
CCHIT	Certification Commission for Health Information Technology
CCOW	clinical context object workgroup
CDO	care delivery organization
CDR	clinical data repository
CEO	chief executive officer
CFO	chief financial officer
CHIME	College of Healthcare Information Management Executives
CIA	Central Intelligence Agency
CIO	chief information officer
CITL	Center for Information Technology Leadership
CLIA	Clinical Laboratory Improvement Amendment
CMIO	chief medical information officer
CMO	chief medical officer
CMS	Centers for Medicare & Medicaid Services
CNO	chief nursing officer
COO	chief operating officer
COW	computer on wheels

CPHIMS	Certified Professional in Healthcare Information Management
CPOE	computerized practitioner order entry
CT	computed tomography
CVIS	cardiovascular information system
DFW	Dallas Forth Worth
DICOM	digital imaging and communications in medicine
DRG	diagnosis related group
ED	emergency department
EDI	electronic data interchange
EFT	electronic funds transfer
EHR	electronic health record
EKG	electrocardiogram
eMAR	electronic medication administration record
EMR	electronic medical record
e-prescribing	electronic prescribing
ERA	electronic remittance advice
FCC	Federal Communication Commission
FDA	U.S. Food and Drug Administration
FEHBP	Federal Employees Health Benefits Program
GDP	gross domestic product
HCMC	Hennepin County Medical Center
HHS	U.S. Department of Health and Human Services
HIE	health information exchange
HIMSS	Healthcare Information and Management Systems Society
HIO	health information organization
HIPAA	Health Insurance Portability and Accountability Act of 1996
HITECH	Health Information Technology for Economic and Clinical Health Act of 2009
HIXNY	Health Information Exchange for New York
HMO	health maintenance organization
HRBO	Health Record Bank of Oregon
HRSA	Health Resources Services Administration
ICD	International Classification of Diseases
ICU	intensive care unit
IDN	integrated delivery network
IMIA	International Medical Informatics Association
IT	information technology
IV	intravenous
LOINC	logical observation identifier name or code
LPN	licensed practical nurse
LVN	licensed vocational nurse

MLA	Medical Library Association
MRI	magnetic resonance imaging
NAHIT	National Alliance for Health Information Technology
NCLEX	National Council Licensure Examination
NGA	National Governors Association
NHIN	Nationwide Health Information Network
NI	nursing informatics
ONC	Office of the National Coordinator for Health Information Technology
OR	operating room
PACS	picture archiving and communication system
PBHR	payer-based health record
PBM	pharmacy benefits management
PC	personal computer
PDA	personal digital assistant
PHR	personal health record
PPO	preferred provider organization
RFID	radio frequency identification
RFP	request for proposal
RHCPP	Rural Health Care Pilot Program
RIS	radiology information system
RN	registered nurse
ROI	return on investment
SIU	Southern Illinois University
SLA	service level agreement
SLO	service level objective
SMART	Specific, Measurable, Attainable, Realistic, and include a Timeframe
SSO	single sign on
TIGER	Technology Informatics Guiding Education Reform
VHA	Veterans Health Administration
WOW	workstation on wheels

Index

A

American Recovery and Reinvestment Act of 2009 (ARRA), xxi, xxii, 24, 26, 100, 102

B

Baylor Health Care System (BHCS), 115–119
Bioelectronics, xxviii–xxix
    smart pumps, xxviii
    ventilators, xxviii

C

Cardiovascular care, xxiv
Centers for Medicare & Medicaid Services (CMS), xx, xxi, xxvii
    consumer-centric health IT, 26
    and diagnosis related group (DRG) payments, xx
    Web site, xxii
Certification Commission for Health Information Technology (CCHIT), xxii, 102
Chief executive officer (CEO), 115–119
    Baldrige planning model, 118–119
    challenges, 119
    goal alignment, 116–118
    leadership role, 116
Chief financial officer (CFO), 31–41
    goal setting, 34
    governance, 35–37
    implementation planning, 40
    operational responsibilities, 37–38
    planning processes, 35
    project management, 39
    project reporting, 40
    role of, 31–32
    value management, 33–34
    vendor relationships, 38–39
Chief information officer (CIO), 1–17, 32
    customer service values, 14–16
    data management, 14
    dimensions and attributes of, 17t
    and executive management, 4–5
    healthcare role, 1–3
    and IT life cycle, 9–10
    IT policy leadership, 4
    IT portfolio appropriateness, 7–12

　　key expectations, 3–16
　　program management, 13
　　recruiting, retention, and mentoring duties, 13–14
　　staff consultation and education, 12
　　strategic direction development, 5–7
Chief medical information officer (CMIO), 57–58
　　responsibilities, 57
　　role of, 58
Chief nursing officer (CNO), 103–104
Clearinghouses, 46–47, 48, 49, 53, 54
Clinical IT, 57–70
　　implementation consequences, 60–61
　　medication reconciliation, 61
　　and transitions of care, 68
　　transformation challenges, 63–66
Clinical Laboratory Improvement Amendment (CLIA), xxiv
Clinical transformation, 87–93
　　and change management, 87–88
　　critical tools of, 90
　　definition of, 88–89
　　governance structure, 90
　　lessons learned, 91–93
　　process map, 91f
Computer provider order entry (CPOE), 103, 104, 105, 107
Consumer setting, 50–51
　　payment solution program, 51
Context management systems, xxvii

D

Data warehousing, xxxiii–xxxiv
Dispensing devices, xxix

E

E-prescribing, 52
Electronic funds transfer (EFT), 50
Electronic health record (EHR), xxii, xxv–xxvii, 59, 89
　　core values, 67–68
　　definition of, xxvi
　　and nursing, 76–77
　　vendor evaluation, 69f
Emergency department, xxv
End-user technologies, xxix–xxxi
Evidence-based core measure set, xxi

F

Financial health information, 43–47
　　clearinghouses, 46–47
　　and electronic-based business practices, 45
　　importance of, 44–45
　　Privacy Rule, 54
　　protection of, 54–55
　　revenue cycle, 44f

H

Health information exchange (HIE), xxxii–xxxiii
Health information technology (IT)
    adoption and use of, 23–25
    benefits of, 20–21
    and consumerism, 25–26
    definition of, 20
    examples of, 20
    hard return on investment, 21, 22t
    soft return on investment, 21t
    and telehealth services, 25
Health Insurance Portability and Accountability Act (HIPAA), xx–xxi, 44, 53–54
Health system, 19–27
    business practices, 22–23
    and consumerism, 25–26
    health IT, 20–22, 23–24
healthcare reform, 26–27
    healthcare spending, 19–20
    and telehealth services, 25
Healthcare continuum, xxiii–xxv
    cardiovascular care, xxiv
    financial applications, xxiv
    medical laboratory and radiology department, xxiv
    registration and scheduling, xxiii
    revenue cycle systems, xxiv
    workflow-driven areas, xxv
Healthcare reform, 26–27, 61–63
Healthcare-enabling technologies, xix
HIMSS Analytics EMR Adoption Model, 23–24
HITECH, xxi, xxiii

I

Institute of Medicine, xx
    To Err is Human: Building a Safer Health System, xx
Institutional provider setting, 47–49
    challenges of, 48
    and financial health IT, 48
    transparency, 48

J

Joint Commission, The, xix, xxi
    accreditation, xxi
    evidence-based core measure set, xxi

K

KLAS Enterprises, LLC, 95–113
    ambulatory EMR, 101–102
    enterprise scheduling, 97
    interfacing, 99
    picture archive and communication system (PACS), 96–97, 102–103
    serving clinicians, 103–112
    software quality study, 100–101

M

Medicaid, 20, 24
Medical laboratory and radiology departments, xxiv
Medical technology, 58
   history of, 59f
Medicare, 20, 24
Medicine
   history, xix–xx

N

Nursing informatics (NI), 71–84
   certification, 81–82
   and clinical decision support, 77
   definition of, 81
   and electronic health records, 76–77
   hardware and software, 78–79
   knowledge workers, 75–76
   nursing process, 71–73
   and patient safety support, 77
   project team, 80–81
   role of, 82
   scope and standards, 81
   staffing considerations, 74–75
   Technology Informatics Guiding Education Reform (TIGER), 82–84
   workflow support, 78
   workforce shortage, 73–74
Nursing process, 71–73
   assessment, 72
   diagnosis, 72
   evaluation, 73
   interventions, 72–73
   outcomes/planning, 72

O

Office of the National Coordinator (ONC), xxi
Office settings, 49–50
   and clearinghouses, 49, 50
   electronic funds transfer, 50
   and insurance claim volume, 49–50
   and transparency, 50
Operating rooms (OR), xxv

P

Patient identification, xxxi
Patient safety, 77
Personal health record (PHR), xxvi–xxvii
Pharmacy setting, 52–53
   and clearinghouses, 53
   e-prescribing, 52
Physicians
   and clinical information technology, 57–70
Picture archiving and communication system (PACS), xxiv, 96–97, 102–103

R

Radio frequency identification (RFID), xxxi–xxxii
Radiology information system (RIS), xxiv
Registered nurse (RN), 74–75
Revenue cycle systems, xxiv, 43–55
    automation challenges, 55
    consumer setting, 50–51
    financial health information, 43–47, 54–55
    institutional settings, 47–49
    office settings, 49–50
    pharmacy setting, 52–53

S

Single sign on (SSO) function, xxvii

T

Technology Informatics Guiding Education Reform (TIGER), 82–84
Telehealth services, 25

V

Value management, 33–34
Veterans Health Administration (VHA), 25–26